THE CUSTOMER WHISPERER

Turning Complaints into Compliments with a Wave of Your Wand

Joan Johnston
Co-Author Raymond Aaron

Foreword by Loral Langemeier, The Millionaire Maker

10-10-10
Publishing

THE CUSTOMER WHISPERER:
Turning Complaints Into Compliments with a Wave of Your Wand
www.thecustomerwhispererbook.com
Copyright © 2024 Joan Johnston

Paperback ISBN: 978-1-77277-637-9

Publisher
10-10-10 Publishing
Markham, ON Canada

Printed in Canada and the United States of America

DEDICATION

To my dearest family,

Stephen Johnston, Herbert & Madge Volney, Richard Johnston, Sheryll, Yordanis, Santi, Yanielle & Yordiel Curet, Natasza Krzyzaniak, Haley Hallet-Johnston, Dominik Bisson, Kaitlyn Johnston, Ariella MacDonald, Evalynah & Milania Johnston, Anne Marie & Ross Tomlinson, Raymond Volney, Thomas & Frances Johnston, Beverly Spence.

This book, *The Customer Whisperer: Turning Complaints into Compliments with the Wave of Your Wand* is dedicated to you, my greatest source of inspiration and support. Your unwavering belief in my vision and your constant encouragement have been the driving forces behind this work. Just as a sturdy tree relies on its roots for strength and nourishment, I have relied on you for guidance and motivation.

From our meaningful conversations to the invaluable lessons we've shared, you have profoundly shaped my approach to exceptional service. Your insights, patience, and encouragement have not only enriched my life but have also inspired me to strive for excellence in every aspect of service to others. Like the steady hand that guides a ship through stormy seas, you have been my compass, helping me navigate through challenges and celebrated my victories.

This book reflects the values we hold dear: dedication, integrity, and a commitment to making a positive impact. It is a tribute to the lessons learned from our collective experiences and the triumphs we have celebrated together. The principles of compassion, love, kindness, efficiency, and excellence that we cherish as a family are woven into the fabric of this book, aiming to inspire others to achieve the same.

Thank you for being my foundation and for instilling in me the drive to pursue this endeavor. Your support has been crucial in shaping my approach and has inspired me to share these insights with others. Your love and belief in me have been the bedrock of my journey, allowing me to build and grow in ways I never imagined.

May this dedication bless you as much as you have blessed me. Your love, support, and belief in me are the greatest gifts I could ever receive. I am forever grateful for each one of you, and I hope this book brings honor to our family's name.

A Lasting Tribute,
With all my love, blessings and gratitude,
Joan

TABLE OF CONTENTS

Testimonials

Raymond Volney, Managing Director, Paradise Properties, St. Lucia Real Estate: *"Joan's book is an essential resource for any professional seeking practical, innovative solutions to enhance customer service and achieve tangible results."*

Anne Marie Tomlinson, DANIER Leather Retiree & YMCA Volunteer: *"The Customer Whisperer" offers actionable insights and strategies that have already improved my team's customer satisfaction. It's a must-read for any business leader seeking to build loyal customer relationships."*

Colin Keddy, RFP, Director of Family Office, TAAG Wealth Management: "Joan's exceptional attention to detail and unwavering professionalism make her stand out in all she does. She embodies the principle that "how you do anything is how you do everything."

Acknowledgments

My deepest gratitude goes out to the many amazing people who have inspired me over the years. I am deeply honored to know you all. You have enriched my life in countless ways, and a simple thank you hardly does you justice. The person I am today reflects your connection, inspiration, and encouragement. You have played a big part in motivating me to write this book. I am profoundly grateful. I apologize if I have unintentionally left anyone out.

A HEARTFELT ACKNOWLEDGMENT TO MY CO-AUTHOR, RAYMOND AARON:

I am profoundly grateful to Raymond Aaron, New York Times Top 10 Bestselling Author, for your invaluable contributions to this book. Your expertise, dedication, and unwavering support have been the backbone of this project. From our first brainstorming sessions to the final revisions, your insights and guidance have elevated this work in ways I could never have imagined. Your commitment to excellence, combined with your creative problem-solving and professional approach, has made this collaboration an absolute joy. You've not only been a brilliant co-author but also a mentor and coach, inspiring me to reach new heights. This book stands as a testament to our shared vision and the incredible journey we've undertaken together. I am deeply honored to have had the opportunity to work with you.

For bonuses go to www.thecustomerwhispererbook.com

THE FACULTY, STAFF & STUDENTS of SIMCOE COUNTY DISTRICT SCHOOL BOARD

THE FACULTY, STAFF & STUDENTS of SIMCOE MUSKOKA CATHOLIC DISTRICT SCHOOL BOARD

THE ONTARIO PUBLIC SECTOR LEADERS and EMPLOYEES of the:
Ministry of Children, Community & Social Services
Ministry of Training, Colleges and Universities

HUMAN SERVICES AGENCIES under the UMBRELLA of:
Solutions Enterprises
Chandelier Pendant

TO SPIRITUAL LEADERS:
St. John Vianney Church: Fr. Joshy George, Fr. K. Biju, Fr. Innocent Okozi
OPS Christian Network: Pastor Frank Loo
The Catholic Women's League / Eucharist Ministers
Knights of Columbus Ladies: JJ Murphy 4th Degree

HEALTH CARE PROVIDERS:
Barrie Community Health Services
Skinsational
ProMotion Health Care
Holly Meadows Chiropractor

Honorable FRIENDS (in alphabetical order):
Andre Winter, Andy & Dorota Fuks, Anell Bennett, Annette Bellamy, Bridget Kemigisa, Caroline Furgiuele, Connie & Graham Surgeno, Daniella Fernandes, Dianne Forsythe, Frank Loo, Gary Harper, Grant & Darlene Snowball, Joanne Willis, Maureen Duncum, Melissa Augustin-DeSouza, Michelle Benjamin, Mike & Sara Jackson, Natasha Dodd-Flake, Nidhi Atri, Pam Pitcher, Ralph Gauthier, Ramzan Khadim, Robert Rotondo, Rosemary Mirigliani, Sarah Whitehall, Tasha Thomas, Vera Poirier

Foreword

As the founder of Integrated Wealth Systems and a New York Times bestselling author, I have read countless books on personal and professional development. *The Customer Whisperer: Turning Complaints into Compliments with a Wave of Your Wand* by Joan Johnston stands out as truly exceptional. This captivating book is a must-read if you are seeking to elevate your customer service skills.

Joan's 50-year career in government and other human services organizations has given her unparalleled access to serving some of the most diverse customer dynamics possible. Her stories and observations illuminate the need for excellence in customer service and the steps you can take to get there.

Written with honesty and candor, Joan includes the unique insights that have formed the cornerstone of her customer experience journey. By comparing customer whispering to horse whispering, you see via analogy and metaphor that often the simplest, most human approach is the most powerful one to take. When you can show up for your customers with kindness, empathy and an authentic desire to truly meet their needs, magic can happen. This is how Joan will inspire you to wave your wand and see the beauty and value of your daily work.

Throughout the book, Joan shares stories from her own life as well as those of her connections as they navigate the path to excellence in customer service. Joan brings a keen eye to the human experience at the heart of every service interaction, showing you how you can bring more understanding and empathy into every customer interaction you have. Every chapter ends with key takeaways, each encouraging you to delve deeper into the material. For Joan, the pursuit of excellence in customer service is a noble and enduring endeavor, and her genuine passion for these shines through every page.

If you are interested in deepening your understanding of the customer-service provider relationship and reaching for excellence in customer service, this is the book for you. Joan's book takes you on an enlightening journey, one that is guaranteed to transform your approach to customer service and leave a lasting impact on your personal and professional life. Even after running successful multimillion dollar companies for years, I found myself learning new things and discovering even more ways to serve my customers with grace and empathy.

Loral Langemeier
The Millionaire Maker

Chapter 1
Understanding Your Customer

"The best way to find yourself is to lose yourself in the service of others."
— Mahatma Gandhi

1

Every once in a while, you make an observation that changes the trajectory of your life. The following story is such a case.

I'm standing in line at the front of the desk at the passport office where I am applying for a passport to go on a honeymoon with my beloved husband in 1973. At the counter standing in line before me is a struggling young mother in her mid-twenties, with tired eyes and slightly tangled hair, standing in the middle of the bustling public office. She has come to the wrong government office and is asking for more money as she is unable to pay her rent and is facing potential eviction.

Her clothes are wrinkled and mismatched, and she is already showing signs of a long, exhausting day. She holds a toddler on her hip, who clings to her shirt with one hand while the other hand reaches out toward the reception counter, trying to grab anything within reach.

Beside her, a second child, maybe around three years old, tugs at her leg, whimpering and pointing to something they want. The child's clothes are slightly dirty, evidence of a spill from earlier in the day. A third baby, still in a stroller, fusses and cries loudly, kicking their legs in frustration, adding to the mother's visible stress.

Her face is flushed with the effort of managing all three children at once. There's a weariness in her expression, but also a sense of determination and love. Despite the chaos surrounding her, she moves with practiced efficiency, quickly shifting from one child to another, trying to meet their needs with limited resources and energy. I can see the remnants of scattered snacks on the stroller, a small toy hanging loosely from the toddler's hand, and a diaper bag slung over her shoulder, heavy with the necessities to care for three young children under the age of four.

I see an exhausted yet resilient mother who is doing her best to manage the overwhelming demands of her young children, all while trying to maintain some semblance of control in a world that, for her, is anything but orderly.

In government, services provided often involve ongoing interaction, such as social services, driver's license or healthcare etc. Referring to individuals as clients rather than "customers" emphasizes the supportive and advisory role the government representative plays, fostering a relationship based on trust and long-term engagement. But at the heart of the engagement remains service, and for the purposes of this book, we'll be using the word "customer" to represent those whom we serve in our work. The young mother is one of dozens of faces I have seen every day in my various lines of work in the human services industry. Although I spent 50 years working with the Ontario Government in Social Services, the stories I share come from various part-time roles I've held across the human services and service-oriented industries. These roles include nurse's aide, residential counselor, personal support worker, supply teacher, education assistant, piano teacher, hotel attendant, social services caseworker, operations manager, superintendent, entrepreneur, volunteer and weekend relief building manager. Any references to the Ontario Government in my stories are derived from publicly available information on the internet, where such details can be accessed by the general public.

I observe as I see the customer service representative (CSR) look the young woman in the eyes as she talks to her, listening intently. Her arms are uncrossed, her body language open. The young mother starts relaxing, and the CSR asks her questions to understand her situation, so she could best advise her in what appears to be in my opinion the most loving and clear way, giving her direction of where to go to get help. In a gentle, compassionate way, she offers to write everything down for her, including drawing a map to follow, after the young mother tells her that she may not remember everything discussed. I listen as the CSR encourages her to read it to her to ensure she understands it. She also gave her a phone number to call before she went there, as she may need to bring paperwork with her. I am impressed with the level of service this federal government employee provided, going over and above the call of duty. I'm hoping that she serves me when it is my turn. This is how I want to be served when I go into any government office, with patience, kindness and dignity.

As is so often the case on days like this, I am reminded of what I learned as a young child who had the occasional opportunity of riding horses, a privilege I earned through volunteer work. The trainers who spoke softly and worked patiently with the horses were the only ones who could break even the wildest, strongest stallions and tame them for riders. The horses never responded to yells, forcing, or punishing consequences. It was whispers that tamed horses, hence the term "horse whisperer." Watching those trainers back then, a young girl with big eyes, felt like watching magic being made. Every time I saw a horse go from bucking someone to calm and gentle, I was convinced the whisperers were magicians.

Now, standing behind a woman, a powerful human with a spirit equally as strong and wild as any horse, I think back to those horse whisperers and how they worked with the horses. I know instinctively that this woman, like every customer I've ever worked with, will respond to whispers, not shouts.

Maintaining a smile and nodding in understanding the CSR listens to the woman who initially rejects her offer in frustration, telling her she will not remember what was said. The patience the older CSR has cultivated through this work knows no limits. It was as though she was also aware that she was role-modeling to the younger girls working nearby. I had the distinct feeling that the mature CSR understood clearly that how she treated the people on the other side of her desks was the most important part of her job, even if she must adhere to policy and legislative boundaries that all government employees must always work within.

For bonuses go to ...

On this day, standing before this woman, the CSR waved her magic wand, not only to meet the immediate needs of this customer but to also ensure she left feeling seen, heard, and reassured. Although she couldn't provide her with additional funds, she was able to connect with the correct government service to obtain the help she needed.

When I left the passport office, I saw the young woman waiting for a bus and I offered her a ride, which she accepted. She mentioned she was a Ukrainian refugee, so I took extra care to introduce her to a network where she could identify and socialize with others who shared her background and experiences, offering her a sense of belonging and understanding. Before she left the car, I noticed her fatigue, and offered her my sandwich and fruit. (I always brought extra food with me to work specifically for this purpose.) She quickly took them and shared them with her children, and it was at that moment I realized she was hungry too. This simple act of sharing and trust in a new country where she, as a refugee, was forced to start a new life, revealed just how deep her need was, beyond what she had expressed.

Since this encounter, stories like this have proliferated in my past, and even today, my wand is ready for waving when empathy, grace and good listening are required. The sad reality is that some customer service representatives have lost their knack for providing exceptional experiences. The repetitive nature of their work has, over time, dulled their ability to empathize and go the extra mile. As a result, some have developed a hardened approach to customer interactions, struggling to demonstrate genuine compassion or understanding.

Where Did Customer Service Go?

In the old days, a business was reliant on its customers. Indeed, the history of business starts with someone solving the problem of someone else, who came to be known as the customer.

xxxx

But over time, and increasingly with the rise of the Internet, customer service has evolved in an unhealthy way. Gone are the days when the phrase, "the customer is always right" was the ultimate guiding principle in customer service, a phrase which, incidentally, was not the complete version and has been used inappropriately for decades. Today, this outdated mindset has been replaced by community forums instead of help desks, Artificial Intelligence (AI) chatbots instead of human operators on the other end of the phone—if customer service exists at all. Massive corporations like Meta and Amazon are notorious for not visibly offering, anywhere in their ecosystems, a clear path to good, old, human-centered customer service. Wait times for customer issues when they call a company are so long that most customers just stop calling, giving them a feeling of helplessness. Communication mix-ups that give companies an advantage over their customers is becoming the norm, not the exception.

In some ways, even someone entirely unfamiliar with the human services world might glance around the online space and deduce that the customer is the lowest person on the food chain, that the businesses themselves are worth more. But this is backwards. The customer is the driving force in a business. How often after serving a customer in the line of duty after an interaction, do clerks thank their customers for coming and tell them to "Have a wonderful day"? Without them, there is no business. The entire existence of human services is to serve the citizens. The people coming in for assistance—whom I'll call customers for the duration of this book—were the only reason public service exists. Human Services employees would not have had a job if it were not for their customers. Just like the brand, Coca-Cola would not have a company were it not for the billions of people reaching for their soda daily.

Customer service should be about more than just providing solutions. It should be about valuing the very people who make the business possible. It's time we remember that, in any business, the customer isn't just important— they are essential. With this mindset you gain a trust and keep yourself focused on what they need. As you assist them, this also gives you a continuing feeling in your heart that you are helping them in some way and giving them a renewed feeling of job satisfaction.

So how have we evolved to this place where customer service has all but vanished, and the lost art of it under threat?

This is why I wrote this book: To revive the art of excellent customer service. I believe this is vital, because no matter whether we're discussing retail, businesses, or government agencies, relationships are what makes the world go around. The relationships you can cultivate with your customers will be how you stand out and differentiate yourself in a world seemingly determined to knock out customer service entirely. My memories of horses and trainers inspired me to see that to excel in customer service perhaps we, too, need to cultivate our own ability to be whisperers—customer whisperers.

My Life In Service

At a very tender age, I learned the profound importance of respecting people less fortunate with love. For the first time, my focus shifted from myself to others, as I was awakened to a world I had never known existed. Growing up in a lower middle class family, my life was centered around my own needs and experiences. But when I first migrated to Canada from the Caribbean at the tender age of 18 fresh out of high school, and away from home for the first time, I embarked on a journey that would forever change my life.

At 19, I met and married my husband, a Canadian from Muskoka, and within a few years, we had two beautiful children. As a biracial family, we settled in a small, picturesque Muskoka community with a population of 2,000 in the early 1970s. The primary sources of employment were a facility for developmentally challenged individuals, a nursing home, several group homes, and a manufacturing plant.

It was during this time that my husband experienced firsthand how people of color were treated differently. When we went shopping together, he saw how store employees would follow me around, watching to see if I was stealing. On one occasion, a pizzeria refused to sell us the pizza we had ordered once they realized we were a biracial family. In another instance, a grocery store clerk refused to accept my cheque, even though my husband regularly paid by cheque without issue.

This is where my passion for enhancing the customer experience began. Living in a community where individuals with developmental challenges made up a large portion of the population, I realized that there were people in this world who were far more vulnerable than I was—people who lacked the capacity to care for themselves in the way I could. This experience shaped my understanding of empathy, service, and the importance of treating everyone with dignity.

Working in a nursing home upon my arrival to Canada, this group of people were my first customers, and through serving them, I learned just how fortunate I was. I realized that life, as I knew it, could change in an instant, and that it was my duty to physically, emotionally, socially and spiritually respect and be kind to everyone, especially those who couldn't care for themselves. This experience not only opened my eyes to the challenges others faced but also instilled in me a deep sense of empathy and responsibility.

I also discovered the value of compassion and patience in dealing with people who depended on others for their well-being and basic needs. It was here that I began to understand the true meaning of service—service that went beyond just fulfilling duties, but one that involved caring for the whole person, understanding their needs, and addressing them with love, kindness and respect.

By the time I was 22, I had internalized the importance of customer service, not as a transaction, but as a relationship. I realized that customer service mattered because it was about making people feel valued, respected, and understood, no matter their circumstances. It was about giving them dignity, even in the smallest interactions.

As I continued in my career, I noticed that this approach to customer service was not always the norm. In many places, the focus was more on efficiency and less on empathy. But I knew from my early experiences that true customer service required a balance of both—serving efficiently while never losing sight of the human connection.

I had a supervisor during those early years who treated me like her own child. She was like a mother to me, guiding me through the complexities of the job and teaching me critical skills that would shape my approach to customer service for the rest of my career. She taught me that every interaction with a customer was an opportunity to make a difference, to leave a positive mark on someone's life, even when no one was looking. Her wisdom and care were instrumental in shaping my values and approach to service.

These early experiences set me on a journey of continuous learning and growth in the field of customer service. They taught me powerful lessons about empathy, responsibility, and the profound impact that genuine care can have on people's lives. As I moved forward in my career, these lessons positioned me as an authority in the field, someone who truly understood the value of serving others with love and compassion.

This all mattered to me because I began to understand the profound difference that genuine care and compassion can make in the lives of others. It was about being fully present and recognizing humanity in every individual I interacted with.

At the nursing home, I remember meeting little Jimmy (the name has been changed to ensure privacy), one of my earliest customers, who taught me the true essence of this calling. Jimmy was a quadriplegic, unable to move or speak, was blind and deaf, and appeared to be incoherent to most people. He had to be fed by a tube, which meant he didn't even have the simple pleasure of tasting his food. To many, he might have seemed unreachable, a person who existed in a world far removed from ours. But to me, Jimmy was a reminder that every person, no matter their condition, deserves to be treated with dignity and love.

I'll never forget the day I had the privilege of spending quiet time with Jimmy. I sat beside him, gently stroking his arm while playing soft, soothing music. To my surprise, I noticed that the expression on his face began to change. The tension in his features eased, and for a brief moment, I caught a glimmer of a smile. It was a small, almost imperceptible change, but it spoke volumes to me. It was as if, in that moment, Jimmy was telling me that he felt seen, cared for, and maybe even a little bit happier.

This experience with Jimmy reinforced why this work mattered so much to me. It wasn't about performing tasks or following procedures. It was about connecting with people on a human level, about understanding their needs, even when they couldn't express them. It was about being there for someone who might not have had anyone else, about offering comfort and companionship in a world that often overlooks those who cannot advocate for themselves.

As I continued in my career, I carried forward the lessons I learned from Jimmy and others like him. I understood the need to deliver excellence in customer service by becoming someone who listens, who notices the small things, who takes the time to connect. I realized that customer service is not just about solving problems; it's about creating moments of care and connection, about making people feel valued and understood, no matter their circumstances.

These experiences shaped my approach to customer service, teaching me that it is as much about heart as it is about skill. It's about the ability to see beyond the surface, to recognize the unspoken needs of others, and to respond with compassion , love and respect. This is why human connection matters to me. I've seen firsthand the difference it can make, not just in the lives of the people we serve, but in our own lives as well. It's a reminder that we are all connected, and that through small acts of kindness, we can bring light and hope into the world.

Inevitably, I became known as the "customer whisperer." For me, being a customer whisperer wasn't merely a title. It was a calling, a way of life that required empathy, patience, and a deep commitment to the well-being of others.

The moniker itself derives from the legacy of horse whisperers, those trainers I mentioned earlier. Horse whisperers are that remarkable subset of humans who transcend the barriers of human-animal communication to form incredibly deep and real bonds with the horses they are trying to help.

The name is fitting as empathy, compassion, connection are at the heart of excellent customer service. Like horse whisperers, a customer whisperer will rely on non-verbal cues to understand the sensations their customer might be experiencing. The customer whisperer will speak gently, attuning to the customer's emotional energy. At the bottom of both horse and customer whispering is the requirement for patience, and caring.

This book will show you how you, too, can become a customer whisperer.

Who is Your Customer?

This book is intended to be read by anyone who works with and for people. For our purposes, we'll call these people "customers," even though it may not be the term that you typically use in your line of work. But whether you work in government, trades, human services (as I did), hospitality, or retail, or whether you are an entrepreneur or work for a large corporation, the message remains the same: good customer service matters.

So, while my experience is rooted in serving the less fortunate, in a variety of capacities, at the end of the day, we are all working with people and striving to help them. In an age where customer service is declining, becoming customer whisperers, whether your customers are actually clients, citizens, volunteers or others, is what truly matters.

Let's define customer. While the more common association with the word "customer" is tethered to business (indeed, most dictionaries offer that as the first definition), for our purposes here we will define customers as being anyone involved in an interaction where goods or services are provided. This includes employees, coworkers, managers, leaders, clients, customers, family, friend, partners, stakeholders, and the public. Every interaction, whether internal or external, is an opportunity to serve and create a positive impact.

True customer service involves providing support before, during, and after any interaction, creating a positive experience that keeps people coming back. This means treating everyone with respect, courtesy, and kindness, even when it's challenging. By recognizing that everyone we interact with is a customer, we can approach each situation with the right mindset—one that values service, respect, and responsiveness.

Understanding who your customers are is the first step towards delivering exceptional service. When I began drafting this book, I considered who I wanted my audience to be. This audience is my customer base for the book. This book is for individuals who work in diverse sectors where customer service is at the heart of what they do.

This includes not only those in retail but also professionals in government agencies and service-based businesses. Having worked in Social Services, Developmental Services and Youth Justice, I know firsthand the challenges and rewards of serving clients in these areas. My audience includes my family, friends, customers, peers, coworkers, managers, colleagues, partners, networks, and all agencies associated with serving our mutual customers.

In every role, where service is provided whether in a service industry, government, education, or retail, we encounter a diverse range of individuals with varying needs and expectations. The comprehensive approach you are about to learn through this book is designed to ensure that every interaction is positive and leaves a lasting impression.

Here are a few ways of understanding and getting to know your customer that I have learned throughout my many years of working in the human services field:

Understand why they are coming in: It's essential to grasp the reason behind a customer's visit. For instance, in government people come in because they have a need, whether it is financial need, or a driver's license or birth certificate etc. This is a very different need than someone casually browsing in a retail store. Understanding this allows you to connect more deeply with the emotions they may be feeling. When people are living below the poverty line and require financial assistance, housing or food, those emotions often include anxiety, nervousness, and desperation. Recognizing these feelings helps you respond with the empathy and care that these situations require.

Understand your own energy and needs: While it's crucial to understand your customer, you must also be aware of your own energy and needs at any given moment. For example, I always knew when it was lunchtime because I would run out of patience faster with my customers. So over time, I learned the importance of staying well-fed and well-hydrated, as well as taking bathroom breaks at appropriate times, so that I could focus completely on the customer needs ensuring that they received the attention and respect they deserved.

Seek to define the customer beyond their surface identity: The rise of identity politics in the world has somehow sent humanity reeling backwards, to an age when people were judged by their skin color, sexuality, or other external markers. These superficial judgments do not reflect the true light of the human inside. It's important to look beyond appearances, whether it's a pink-haired, or a tattooed teenager, or someone who looks completely different from you. Instead of labeling or judging them based on their looks, attune to their energy, non-verbal cues, and other signs of their humanity. This approach helps you connect on a deeper level and provides a more meaningful and respectful service experience.

The Importance of Customer Expectations

These tools are not just strategies for better customer service, they are principles for creating a more inclusive and understanding world. My experiences, like the one at the pizzeria, the insensitive questions at work about my background when people met me for the first time, were some of the moments that have shaped my approach to service and reinforced the importance of seeing each customer as a whole person, deserving of dignity and respect, regardless of their background or appearance. By applying these principles, we can all contribute to a more compassionate and connected society.

Customers come to us with specific expectations, shaped by their past experiences and their current needs. These expectations can include being treated with courtesy, receiving timely and accurate information, and experiencing a sense of being valued and understood. Meeting these expectations is essential, but going beyond them is what creates memorable and positive experiences.

For example, I've encountered situations where female customers who have been physically or sexually abused come into my office and ask if they can speak with a woman, hesitant to be served by a man. Their expectation is rooted in their need for safety and comfort, and understanding this allows us to accommodate their request, ensuring they feel secure and respected.

In other instances, customers with disabilities or language barriers require special accommodation. For a deaf customer, this might mean communicating in writing. For a visually impaired person, it could involve providing information in large print or audio format. Language barriers might require a translator app or an interpreter who can communicate in the customer's preferred language. Additionally, physical accessibility is crucial—customers in wheelchairs may need lower counters, wheelchair-accessible doors, or door openers. Even something as simple as providing larger chairs for bigger individuals can make a significant difference in their comfort and experience.

Understanding and managing customer expectations is crucial. When customers feel that their needs are understood and met, their trust and satisfaction increase. This not only enhances their individual experience but also strengthens their overall confidence in the services provided. By taking the time to understand and anticipate these expectations, we position ourselves to deliver outstanding service consistently.

Anticipating Customer Needs

Becoming a customer whisperer means understanding your customer so deeply that you can anticipate their needs, even when they don't explicitly explain them.

When a customer makes an unusual request, it's important to recognize that we may not fully understand their situation. If their request can be met without creating a burden for the organization, why not do so?

For example, when a female customer asks to be served by a female staff member, there is likely a significant reason behind the request. Respecting this acknowledges the customer's need for comfort and safety. Some customers may not want to explain the personal reasons for their requests. To them, it is not unusual but necessary based on their experiences.

We also need to recognize that some disabilities are invisible and may require special accommodations. A person with claustrophobia, for instance, could become agitated if placed in a small room. Understanding that these unspoken, subtle needs may exist allows us to respond appropriately and offer the right support without question.

Anticipating customer needs varies depending on the work. In my experience, it involved looking beyond immediate requests to understand deeper needs and future requirements. This proactive approach enabled us to deliver timely and forward-thinking solutions.

For example, in the hospitality industry where I briefly worked part-time, we prepare for seasonal spikes in reservations. During the hockey season, anticipating an increase in hotel reservations helped us staff up, provide additional training, and update resources to handle the surge efficiently. This ensured that guests received optimum service without delays.

Anticipating needs also involves personalizing our approach. In retail or business settings, it is similar to how social media platforms predict what you want to watch or how Netflix queues up for the next show. By paying attention to cues and feedback, we can tailor responses to suit each customer's unique situation. This level of care turns good service into exceptional service, building trust and long-term satisfaction.

Each customer interaction is unique, and by paying attention to individual cues and feedback, we can tailor our responses to better suit their specific situations. This level of attention and care is what transforms good service into exceptional service, fostering trust and long-term satisfaction.

Top Three Takeaways

Understand Your Customer: Recognize that everyone you interact with is a customer, from friends, family, colleagues to community members. By viewing each person through the lens of service, love and respect, you can foster more positive and productive interactions.

Anticipate and Exceed Expectations: Customers expect courtesy, timely information, and to feel valued. By understanding and anticipating these needs, you can create memorable experiences that build trust and satisfaction, ensuring you're always prepared for future challenges.

Master Stakeholder Management: Effective service delivery relies on strong stakeholder relationships. Regular communication, active listening, and collaboration help you gather valuable insights and improve service. This interconnected approach enhances both individual experiences and the broader service impact.

Make every customer feel valued and heard, waving your hand and turning their concerns into praise, like the thoughtful customer whisperer you are.

Chapter 2
The Magic of Listening

*"Most people do not listen with the intent to understand;
they listen with the intent to reply."*
– Stephen R. Covey, *The 7 Habits of Highly Effective People*

2

I n the world of horse whispering, one of the first things a whisperer often does is known as the "join-up technique." The technique was designed to build trust and connection between horse and trainer. Among the steps in this technique are creating a controlled environment and from there, the whisperer controls the horse's behavior.

This observation is done softly, gently, silently. The trainer is watching the horse to determine the horse's level of comfort and trust, and to understand the horse's state of mind. After a while, the trainer themselves may start to mirror the horse, thereby increasing trust and comfort.

When we can stand in silence before our customers and listen deeply to their concerns, we are engaging in our own version of customer whispering.

Silence can be a powerful tool. In a world where everyone is eager to be heard, taking the time to genuinely listen sets you apart. Imagine a bustling coffee shop, filled with the hum of conversation. Amid the noise, a waitress or receptionist who pauses, looks into your eyes, and truly listens to your order, stands out. That moment of silent presence shows respect and builds a connection.

In customer service, that same principle applies. Being present and silent allows you to absorb not just the words, but the emotions and intentions behind them. It's like tuning into a hidden frequency, where the real message often lies. Staying silent just that much longer and attuning to the body language and non-verbal cues of the person before you are how you wave your wand to harness the magic within to transform complaints into heartfelt compliments.

Hearing Beyond Words

In the bustling atmosphere of a residential apartment complex, the sounds of quiet conversations, the occasional ringing of phones, people coming and going, and the soft hum of washing machines and dryers filled the air on a typical Saturday morning. My husband and I were working as weekend relief building managers, a role where people often sought help, guidance, or sometimes simply a friendly chat. The morning had been a whirlwind of activity, with residents and visitors from all walks of life passing through the doors. Then, a woman entered, searching for housing.

Diana (the name changed for confidentiality) was young, perhaps in her mid-twenties, but her eyes carried the weight of someone who had seen far more than her years should allow. As she entered, I noticed her quick, almost furtive steps, her eyes scanning the room as if searching for an escape route. Her body language screamed unease—her shoulders hunched forward, her arms crossed tightly over her chest, and her fingers restlessly twirling a strand of hair.

As she approached the office, where I provided evening and weekend relief, I couldn't help but notice the visible signs of distress. A large bruise darkened the side of her face, and her lower lip was swollen and split. Her hands, which clutched her purse tightly, bore the faint purple marks of bruises around her wrists. She looked like someone who had been through something traumatic, but I didn't know what it was—yet.

Diana began speaking before I had a chance to greet her, her words coming out in a hurried, jumbled stream. The content of her request was vague—she needed help with some paperwork, but she was clearly struggling to articulate what exactly she needed. There was something more beneath her words, a tension, an unspoken fear that seemed to weigh heavily on her.

Hearing beyond words, I leaned in slightly, focusing not just on what she was saying but how she was saying it. Her voice was strained, her sentences clipped, and I could sense that the issue she was presenting was only the tip of the iceberg. Beneath the surface, I could feel a storm of emotions swirling—anxiety, fear, perhaps even desperation.

"Diana, take your time," I said gently, my voice calm and steady. "We're here to help you with whatever you need."

She hesitated, her eyes flicking up to meet mine for a brief moment before darting away again. There was a slight tremble in her voice as she continued, but now she was speaking a bit more slowly, a bit more deliberately. As she did, I watched her closely—her fidgeting hands, the way she bit her lower lip, the tension in her shoulders. The visible bruises were concerning, but I didn't want to jump to conclusions. I needed to understand her situation fully.

When she finished speaking, I didn't respond right away. Instead, I asked a few gentle questions, probing just a little deeper, trying to uncover the emotions she was guarding so closely. "It sounds like this has been really stressful for you," I said, my tone full of empathy. "Can you tell me more about what's been going on?"

The question hung in the air for a moment, and I could see the conflict in her eyes. She looked down at her hands, her fingers still trembling slightly. "I... I just... I don't know what to do anymore," she whispered, her voice barely audible. "Everything's falling apart, and I'm so scared."

I leaned in a bit closer, keeping my tone gentle and non-threatening. "It's okay, Diana. You don't have to go through this alone. We're here to support you, whatever you're facing."

For a moment, she didn't say anything. Then, she took a deep, shaky breath and looked up at me, her eyes filled with tears. "It's... it's my partner," she finally admitted, her voice trembling. "He's been... he's been hurting me. I thought I could handle it, but last night... last night was too much."

The pieces started to fall into place. The bruises, the fear in her eyes, the way she seemed to be constantly looking over her shoulder—it all made sense now. Diana was a victim of domestic abuse, and she had finally reached her breaking point.

I nodded, my heart aching for her. "Thank you for telling me, Diana," I said softly. "You've been incredibly brave. Now let's make sure you get the help you need."

Having firsthand knowledge of local community resources from my other human services work, I quickly connected her with a local women's shelter where she could find refuge, but I knew that wasn't enough. She needed legal protection as well. "I'm going to refer you to Legal Aid," I told her. "They can help you apply for a restraining order against your partner, which will legally prevent him from coming near you. It's an important step in keeping you safe."

I made the call to Legal Aid on her behalf, explaining her situation and arranging for an urgent appointment. They would assist her in filing the necessary paperwork for a restraining order, ensuring she had the legal protection to keep her abuser away.

I then referred her to Social Services to apply for emergency financial assistance. This would give her some immediate funds to cover her basic needs. I also provided information about a support group for survivors of domestic abuse and connected her with a healthcare clinic where she could get the medical attention she desperately needed. As a housing building manager, this was over and above the call of my duties, but I could not just send her away on a Friday afternoon of a long weekend.

As we worked through the steps, I could see the tension slowly ebbing away from her body. Her hands steadied, her voice grew calmer, and the nervous tapping of her nails ceased. By the time we were finished, Diana looked like a different person—still burdened, but no longer on the verge of breaking.

"Thank you," she said softly as she gathered her things. "I feel... better now. Like I can handle this."

I smiled, feeling a sense of fulfillment. "Remember, Diana, I am here every weekend if you need me. Don't hesitate to reach out."

As she walked out, her steps were slower, more measured, and I could see the faintest hint of a smile on her face. It wasn't just about solving her problem. It was about seeing her, hearing her, and understanding the unspoken fears that had been weighing her down.

In this line of work, it's easy to get caught up in the procedures, the paperwork, and the checklists. But sometimes, the most important service we can offer is simply to listen—not just to the words our customers say, but to the emotions and needs hidden beneath them. It's about hearing beyond words and responding with empathy, patience, and understanding. That's where true connection—and true service—begins.

Active Listening Techniques

The art of listening is often one that is taken for granted, and for people outside of customer-facing service work, it's often not something they even consider.

Within the art of listening is a style of listening known as "active listening." Active listening doesn't just include hearing; it includes active engagement with the person you are listening to.

Imagine a conversation with a person who is listening to you while scrolling on their phone. How does it feel to talk with a person who is distracted, only half-listening? Usually it feels annoying, and almost always, we feel unheard.

Contrast this now by imagining you're having a conversation with a friend who nods as they listen. Then, they repeat back to you what they heard. Even better, they interject periodically to ask a clarifying question or two. How might this feel?

Most people will agree that the latter kind of conversation leaves them feeling valued and understood. In customer service, using techniques like active listening (listening with full intention to understand) and reflective listening (listening and then repeating the customer's words back to them) can make a huge difference. Below is a short list of simple phrases you can use that show the customer that you're fully engaged. It's about making them feel heard and seen as humans, not just units being processed.

Phrases I've Learned to Use While Active Listening:

- "What I'm hearing you say is..."
- "It sounds to me like you are feeling... Is that correct?"
- "I understand. That must feel ..."
- "Tell me more about how that feels."
- "It sounds like you're really concerned about ..."
- "Help me understand what you're experiencing right now."
- "It must have been really frightening when that happened."
- "I'm hearing that this has been really difficult for you."
- "Can you walk me through how that's affecting you?"
- "Let's explore what's on your mind a bit more."
- "I'm here to listen, so feel free to share more about what you're feeling."

Why Relationships Matter

Relationships are the foundation of our existence, woven into the very fabric of what it means to be human. From the moment we enter the world, relationships become the lifeline that sustains us. As infants, we rely on our parents or caregivers to meet our most basic needs, not just for food and shelter, but for love, comfort, and security. This connection is vital for our survival and development. It is through these early relationships that we learn to trust, to communicate, and to understand our place in the world.

As we grow, relationships continue to shape our lives. They are the channels through which we experience joy, love, and companionship, but also through which we face challenges, learn resilience, and grow as individuals. The quality of our relationships often determines the quality of our lives. Whether it's family, friends, colleagues, or even brief encounters with strangers, every interaction we have contributes to our understanding of ourselves and the world around us.

In essence, relationships are the threads that connect us to others and to the broader human experience. They are not just about social bonds. They are about connection, meaning, and shared experiences. Relationships remind us that we are part of something greater than ourselves, and they provide the context within which we live our lives.

When we consider relationships in the context of customer service, the same principles apply. Just as we seek connection and understanding in our personal lives, customers seek these things in their interactions with businesses. A relationship with a customer is not merely transactional. It's a connection built on trust, respect, and mutual understanding. When customers feel seen, heard, and valued, it transforms the interaction from a mere exchange of goods or services into a meaningful experience.

Customers want to know that they matter, that their needs and concerns are important. This is why building and nurturing relationships with customers is so crucial. It goes beyond providing a product or solving a problem. It's about creating a connection that leaves the customer feeling valued and respected. This connection fosters loyalty encourages repeat business, and often turns customers into advocates who will sing your praises to others.

In a world where many interactions are increasingly impersonal and automated, the power of a strong, human-centered relationship cannot be overstated. By focusing on the relationship, you demonstrate that your business cares not just about the bottom line, but about the people who contribute to it. This approach not only enhances customer satisfaction but also builds a foundation of trust that can withstand challenges and competition.

In summary, relationships are at the heart of the human experience, essential to our survival and well-being. In the realm of customer service, they are equally critical. By prioritizing and nurturing relationships with customers, businesses can create lasting connections that lead to success, loyalty, and a positive impact that resonates far beyond a single transaction.

Where are you in relationship? With whom?

The first relationship you may observe is the one with yourself. How is that relationship? Do you tend to it and care for it? Or is it always being neglected?

Your other relationships around you might be your family, your partner and children, or your pets. You engage in relationship with these people nearly every hour of the day when you are together. What is the quality of these relationships like? Some people emphasize their relationships greatly and make every effort to keep them thriving. But many others take relationships for granted, likely because they are such a staple of life, we barely notice them.

Then there are the relationships we have with nature, the inanimate (or animate?!) world around us. How is your relationship with the grass in your yard? You might mow it and tend to it with love and care. What about your relationship with your pet? You might take care to feed your cat, dog, fish or bird quality food and ensure they get lots of play, because you care about the relationship you have with your beloved pet.

Relationships surround us and affect us nearly every moment of every day. This is why the most business-minded of the business-minded know that at the heart of business and commerce are relationships. This is true of government as well, although there is a different feeling attached to public service relationships. Businesses and governments share a mutually dependent relationship with their customers. Business owners rely on customers for the revenue that sustains their operations. Similarly, governments depend on citizens, whose taxes fund public sector wages. This interdependence highlights the essential role each plays in the success of the other. Neither can thrive without the other.

People from all walks of life have shared their experiences with the services provided at different levels of government—federal, provincial, and municipal. A common theme is the presence of signage and outgoing messages in public service offices, doctors' offices, and even on public transit, urging citizens to show kindness and patience toward staff. These reminders seem to point to an underlying tension in the relationship between the public and human services. Many have observed that such requests likely wouldn't be needed if frustration and dissatisfaction weren't so widespread.

Citizens often feel that their concerns are not being adequately addressed, leading to a sense of disempowerment and frustration. This, in turn, has prompted government and some business offices to request patience and understanding, creating a cycle where both sides feel increasingly disconnected and dissatisfied.

Increasingly, too, many customers of retail business feel disempowered in the face of companies pulling back efficient customer service options in the modern world. Chat forums simply cannot replace the voice of a knowledgeable human.

Humans can never be replaced by artificial intelligence, robots, or automation in customer service because the essence of excellent customer service lies in building relationships. Think about your favorite local bakery. It's not just the delicious pastries that keep you coming back, but the warm smile of the baker who knows your name and your favorite treat. Building relationships with customers creates loyalty and trust. These relationships turn one-time interactions into repeat engagements and advocates for your service. It's like tending to a garden—when you give it care and attention, it flourishes and grows.

Keep in mind, many people feel vulnerable considering it this way. I recognize that not everyone in a customer-facing job is up to the task of opening their hearts, developing the empathy they need, and showing up with excellence. Some staff may be in situations just as challenging as those of their customers, dealing with poverty, illness, or even abusive relationships, all while working in low-paying jobs. Low wages can significantly impact a person's motivation and ability to rise above their own struggles. Imagine a young mother, struggling to make ends meet while working a retail sales job at a clothing store. On some days, it may be incredibly difficult for her to elevate her work and fully engage with customers when she's burdened by her own stresses, feeling overwhelmed and underpaid.

Remember, taking care of yourself is essential to serving others effectively. Who you are is valuable and already complete. While you can continue to develop the skills needed to build quality relationships, it's important to recognize that this isn't rocket science, nor is it a complex plan or something requiring a degree. The most important thing is to be open to seeing the person across from you as a fellow human, with their own thoughts, emotions, and life experiences, just like you. The relationship doesn't have to be intimate or deep, but it does need to be acknowledged and respected. This is how true connection is made—and connection lies at the heart of excellent customer service.

The Heart of Customer Service

Customer service is more than just solving problems. It's about building meaningful connections between people. When you reach out for support and are met with a friendly, empathetic voice that truly cares about your concerns, it creates an experience that transcends mere transactions. Good customer service benefits both the service provider and the customer.

For the customer, it fosters a sense of being valued and respected, turning a routine interaction into something memorable. For the provider, it offers the satisfaction of making a positive impact, reinforcing the importance of empathy and human connection. This exchange creates a lasting impression that enriches both sides, making the experience truly worthwhile.

The challenge in modern life is to get to that human voice in the first place. Nearly every tech company and e-commerce company with significant online presence has reduced customer service to bots and forums. It's nearly impossible to speak with a human at most companies. Many public service agencies are also starting to do this, moving their services and infrastructure increasingly to online or automated processes. Parallel this with the rise of a generation of kids raised on texting and iPads, afraid to phone people or even talk on the phone at all. Are we at risk of losing the heart of customer service? It's possible.

This is how small businesses may have an advantage, however. Internet fatigue is growing all over as people recognize that what was promised to be the ultimate in connecting us simply doesn't. After all, if social media was truly connecting people, would we really be seeing the amount of division the modern age is full of?

Government services are mandated to remain accessible, and because of this there is a higher chance that government services will always be made available in person or over the phone with a human. But it's clearly evidenced that large companies and corporations are shaving their margins by diminishing the expense of quality customer service, leaving a gap for small local businesses to step in. People are hungry for connection. The small local retailer who gives a smile, asks how you are, and is ready to help you when you need it, is the retailer who will have a ready flock of happy customers at all times.

Nurturing Positive Relationships Every Day

Building strong customer relationships is an ongoing process. This can only be done by treating customers with dignity, respect, kindness, and courtesy. It's like maintaining any relationship. It requires consistent effort and genuine care.

Showing up fully and with presence often begins with self-care and being present with ourselves. It's a tall order to remain kind, respectful, and courteous to everyone throughout your shift, especially when faced with challenging situations. The man who was rude to you still needs to be treated with kindness. The noisy child who's making it difficult to assist their mother requires gentle guidance, not frustration. The woman asking the same questions repeatedly because she's struggling with early-stage dementia deserves patience, empathy, and courtesy.

These situations can be particularly challenging for those who may not feel strong in themselves or who find it difficult to separate their own needs and triggers from the task at hand. A customer's behavior might trigger strong emotions in a service provider, but it's essential to stay calm and composed, responding rather than reacting. This is the work of personal growth, the practice of building relationships that are both sustainable and fulfilling for everyone involved.

By practicing patience and persistence in these moments, we not only become better at handling our own challenges, but we also grow stronger in the process. The key is to approach these situations as opportunities for growth rather than obstacles. Sometimes, all a customer-facing service provider needs is to cultivate healthy relationships in their personal lives first. The strength and positivity from these relationships can then ripple out into their interactions with others, making their service more genuine and impactful. Alternatively, cultivating healthy relationships at work with customers, where they spend most of their day, can positively influence their personal lives as well, creating a virtuous cycle of growth and connection.

Every interaction is an opportunity to strengthen the bond. Simple gestures, like following up on a previous issue or remembering a customer's preference, show that you value them as individuals. Over time, these small acts accumulate, creating a foundation of trust and loyalty. It's the everyday moments that build lasting relationships and turn customers into lifelong supporters. With a nurturing wave of your magical wand, you too can turn frustration into appreciation. Here is such a story:

The building manager's office was bathed in the soft glow of early morning light filtering through the blinds on a Saturday morning. It was the kind of morning that made you believe the day would be uneventful, even serene. The air was filled with the usual sounds of ringing phones, the quiet hum of conversations, and the rhythmic tapping of washing machines. Contractors scattered across the building were beginning to sink into their day's work, focused and calm.

At 8:39 a.m., the calm was broken by a sudden, violent crash. The sound was unmistakable—something heavy and forceful. It echoed through the main floor, leaving everything in silence. I jumped from my chair, heart racing, and hurried out of my office. As I turned the corner, I was met with complete chaos.

A man, disheveled and wild-eyed, had forced his way into the building through the secure entrance, the door now hanging loosely on its hinges, the alarm blaring in an ear-piercing wail. He was tall, with a broad frame, wearing a tattered coat that had seen better days. His hair was matted, and his face was twisted in a mix of anger and desperation. His eyes, bloodshot and darting around frantically, seemed to lock onto every person he passed, as if searching for something or someone.

He moved with frantic energy, his steps heavy and erratic, each one leaving behind a trail of fear. As he charged forward, his arms flailed wildly, and in his wake, three residents stepping out of the elevator were down, clutching at the spots where he had struck them. Their expressions were a mix of pain and terror, eyes wide with disbelief, as they struggled to comprehend what had just happened.

Panic spread like wildfire through the building. Onlookers who had been quietly passing through the halls moments before were now scrambling to their feet, eyes wide, hands shaking. Plants and furniture were overturned as people tried to back away, to find some sense of safety in a small space. Some froze, rooted to the spot by fear, while others fumbled for their phones, their trembling fingers dialing for help.

Shouts filled the air, frantic cries that only added to the chaos. "Pull the fire alarm," someone yelled. "Call the police!" another voice echoed, rising above the din. The sound of the alarm, the shouts, and the panicked movements created a scene that was spiraling out of control.

But amidst the chaos, I knew I had to act. My heart pounded in my chest, every instinct screaming at me to panic, to join the rush to safety. But years of experience had taught me one crucial lesson: silence and calm were the keys. I forced myself to breathe deeply, to steady my racing thoughts.

A whistle blew, and in an instant, the building went into automatic lockdown. I looked around and saw that many of us had taken refuge in a large boardroom. Fear was evident in everyone's eyes, but so was a sense of determination. We were shaken, but we were together. In that moment, I realized that the calm we had created, however fragile, was the first step toward navigating through the crisis. The building had been a flurry of movement, whispers, and urgent gestures. But then, an eerie silence settled over the lobby.

Through overhead mirrors, we could see the intruder, wild-eyed and breathing heavily, as he sensed the shift in the atmosphere. He paused, his eyes darting around the now quiet lobby. People had either locked themselves in their main floor apartments or hid, leaving the space eerily deserted.

For a moment, he stood there, chest heaving, unsure of what to do. His confusion grew as he found only empty spaces and closed doors. Slowly, he began to backtrack, his footsteps echoing in the silence. His gaze lingered on the overturned furniture and scattered plants before he headed toward the door, he had forced open.

The tension in the air was palpable, every breath held by those still hiding, hoping, praying that he wouldn't turn back. Looking through the overhead mirrors, I saw his gaze sweep over the lobby one last time, lingering on the overturned furniture and scattered plants that told the story of his brief but violent intrusion.

Then, with a final glance, he turned and made his way back toward the door he had initially forced open. His steps were less frantic now, more deliberate, as if the fight had drained out of him, leaving only a hollow shell of the man who had stormed in minutes earlier. The door creaked as he pushed it open again, the sound eerily loud in the silence.

At the threshold, he hesitated but then stepped through, retreating from the building. The damaged door remained slightly ajar, leaving the oppressive silence to settle once more, broken only by the fading sound of his footsteps.

Slowly, people emerged from their hiding spots, pale and wide-eyed, as the reality of what had happened began to sink in. The building, once lively, now felt like a battlefield after a brief, intense skirmish.

I stood catching my breath, watching people reassemble with a mix of fear and relief. Though the intruder was gone, the impact of his presence still lingered, a reminder of how quickly chaos can disrupt order.

The rest of the day was a blur of urgency and careful management. The initial chaos had given way to a tense calm, leaving the building eerily quiet.

In the aftermath, the silence that had protected us during the lockdown remained crucial. It was not just the absence of sound but a collective understanding that any noise could have worsened the situation. Everyone knew their safety depended on staying silent and composed.

As the building manager on duty, my priority was ensuring the safety of my customers, the residents. Despite the adrenaline, I stayed calm, quietly texting building security with details and directing them to block all access points. My clear, quiet communication kept the residents focused and prevented further escalation.

My role in the recovery focused on ensuring my residents' safety and well-being while guiding them through the aftermath. I coordinated with emergency services, and informed head office of what had happened. Recognizing the trauma's impact, I posted a local crisis hotline number for anyone who wanted or needed it. I immediately called contractors to do repairs, and conducted a physical assessment of the building to check for any other potential danger or hot spots. To support the residents, I remained available maintaining regular check-ins to monitor their well-being.

In addition to the logistical and emotional support, I focused on strengthening coherence by fostering an environment of empathy and mutual support. My leadership during the crisis, grounded in the principles of the customer whisperer, inspired the residents to come together in solidarity. They took it upon themselves to collect funds to purchase flowers for the assaulted residents recovering in their units. This act of kindness not only comforted those who were injured but also reinforced the bond among the residents.

The actions of the tenants mirrored the values of compassion and care that I had consistently demonstrated. By leading with empathy and composure, I helped foster a culture where residents supported and comforted one another in meaningful ways. This sense of community strengthened their resolve, transforming a traumatic event into an opportunity for deeper connection and resilience. Both corporate leadership and fellow residents recognized our collective efforts, highlighting the importance of leading with empathy, care, and resilience, even in the most challenging circumstances.

In the aftermath of the crisis, it became clear that my residents were not just tenants; they were the customers I needed to care for most at that moment. The principles of hearing beyond words, paying attention to their tone of voice, their body language, and other non-verbal cues were crucial in understanding the depth of their trauma and guiding them through the recovery.

After the crisis, the residents were understandably shaken, their movements hesitant and confidence fragile. This was not a time for grand gestures but for quiet nurturing, focusing on gently rebuilding the sense of safety and trust that had been disrupted.

As a customer whisperer, I understood that healing would come from small, continuous and consistent acts of care and support. It was about reconnecting with each individual, offering reassurance through empathy, and creating a space where everyone felt safe, secure, seen, heard, and valued. By fostering this environment, we could slowly rebuild the trust that is essential for our residents to thrive and for our service to continue meeting the needs of those we serve.

For bonuses go to ...

Forming a connection is ultimately what this is all above, and the connection is what becomes the backbone of the relationship. When horse whisperers mirror the horse in the join-up process, they are building that connection. I recall seeing this once in my childhood, and it was marvelous to watch. The trainer began mirroring the actions of the horse, and before long it was hard to tell who was mirroring whom in the dance. It was a powerful moment. There, in the silent corral, a horse was learning to connect with a human.

Top Three Takeaways

The magic of listening lies in its ability to transform customer interactions into meaningful connections, showing that truly listening to customers can create profound impacts.

As a customer whisperer, **active listening is your most powerful tool,** allowing you to understand the true needs and emotions of those you serve.

By waving your wand of attentive and compassionate listening, you can **build and nurture relationships that foster trust,** loyalty, and long-term satisfaction.

Make every customer feel valued and heard, waving your hand and turning their concerns into praise, like the thoughtful customer whisperer you are.

Chapter 3
Building the Right Mindset

"People will forget what you said, people will forget what you did, but people will never forget how you made them feel."

– Maya Angelou

3

The reason horse whispering is so profoundly effective is because it is designed to subtly as well as overtly improve communication in a way that enhances trust and thus increases safety for both horse and rider.

Any good horse whisperer will tell you that the right mindset is essential for the work. Charging forward and meeting a stallion's wild fiery energy with a similar fire will simply not work. Instead, the whisperer becomes malleable like water.

This is what a good customer whisperer does, too, and with the right mindset, they can achieve that quality of water, that fluidity required in the face of a fiery customer. This is the magic wand you wave. When you respond with compassion, you are waving this wand and when this happens you transform a complaint into a genuine "thank you "or compliment.

To become fluid, like water, it is essential that we care for ourselves. The horse whisperer who does not care for themselves effectively can never seek to achieve the calm state required when working with such wild beasts. Self-care also informs our ability to develop empathy and kindness, in the sense that self-care is designed to bring us more energy. Energy we can then use to respond with grace even in our most exhausted, end-of-the-day moments.

Horse whisperers understand the power of caring for themselves and how this affects the work they do. At the end of it all is trust. The relationship between the whisperer and the horse is built on trust, which is the foundation of their bond.

The Power of Self-Care and Positive Thinking

Self-care is what sets the foundation of a positive mindset, something that is especially helpful when working in roles that involve constant interaction with the public. While there are lots of opinions around self-care in society, the most obvious example supporting the value and necessity of self-care arises in the old airplane scenario. You must put your oxygen mask on first before you can help others. This is the basis of self-care. Fill your cup first, so that you can give from the overflow.

What does self-care look like? It looks different for everyone. Imagine starting your day with a clear mind, feeling refreshed and ready to tackle any challenge. Taking time for yourself, whether it's through exercise, meditation, or simply a quiet moment with a cup of tea, can set a positive tone for your day. This kind of self-care sets the stage for positive thinking, enabling you to approach every interaction with a clear and open mind. When you take care of yourself, you are better equipped to take care of others.

Positive thinking isn't about ignoring challenges but about approaching them with a constructive attitude. It's about seeing opportunities where others see obstacles and believing in your ability to make a difference. By maintaining a positive outlook, you not only improve your own well-being but also create a more uplifting environment for your colleagues and the people you serve.

Both self-care and positive thinking are often connected to an individual's experience of spirituality. Our spiritual beliefs are unique and private to each of us, but they are often a source of strength we can draw from, which comes in handy when interacting with other humans in an otherwise transactional experience.

Personally, my spiritual beliefs infuse every single thing I do, even the writing of this book. I believe that my spirituality is key to my ability to serve with grace, empathy and depth. So, for me, self-care includes regular devotional practices, along with my weekly visit to church. My spiritual beliefs have formed the foundation of my life, and allowed me access to greater empathy and kindness, both of which we will discuss later in this chapter.

I have brought my spirituality into the workplace with me because it is a core component of my being; everything I do is infused with my spiritual beliefs. Sometimes, I may be overt about this, as you'll see below in the story of MM. Other times, I wait and watch for cues the customer is open to that level of dialogue; if so, I ask an inviting question. If not, I simply emanate spirit by virtue of my being, my approach to the interaction, how I am in the moment.

Bridging Spirituality with Customer Service

In today's diverse and interconnected world, the role of spirituality in customer service is both delicate and profound. While society often separates spirituality from business interactions, there is a way to infuse our spiritual values into customer service without crossing boundaries or causing discomfort.

It's essential to approach spirituality in a manner that honors both our beliefs and the beliefs of those we serve. The key is not to verbalize or impose our spiritual views but to let our spirituality guide our actions. For instance, rather than discussing religious figures or practices, which might unintentionally offend a customer of a different faith or background, we should focus on embodying the qualities that our spiritual beliefs inspire in us, compassion, patience, understanding, and respect.

By fortifying ourselves with the grace and wisdom of our spiritual beliefs, whether rooted in God, a higher power, or a broader cosmology, we can create an environment where our actions speak louder than words. Our interactions should reflect the kindness, empathy, and integrity that our spirituality teaches us, allowing customers to feel valued and respected without feeling pressured or alienated by discussions of faith.

Ultimately, the most respectful and effective way to integrate spirituality into customer service is to let it shine through in our deeds, ensuring that every customer feels supported, understood, and treated with dignity, regardless of their spiritual background.

Cultivating Empathy and Kindness

MM was a young man who, at first glance, seemed to have everything in order. He was well-groomed and handsome, with clean, well-kept clothes and a neatly trimmed haircut. His quiet demeanor gave no indication of the emotional turmoil brewing beneath the surface. Despite his composed appearance, MM was silently battling an invisible disability—severe depression—that made social interactions difficult and overwhelming.

Whenever MM visited the apartment building office where he lived, his distress was evident. His eyes were often red from crying, his hands trembled slightly, and he struggled to express his needs. His emotions frequently overpowered him, leading to episodes of frustration and tears. Unfortunately, Sean (name changed), the 25-year-old first-time building manager fresh out of college with a degree in Property Management, was not fully prepared to address MM's unique challenges. Using standard communication methods, Sean inadvertently heightened MM's confusion and distress.

Without a compassionate, tailored approach, MM felt unheard and unsupported, trapped in a cycle where his issues remained unresolved. Each visit ended the same way, leaving him in despair, only to return in the same state of confusion, searching for help that never came.

After several unsatisfied visits, MM's tears and frustration grew more pronounced, and he requested to speak with head office. When I heard this, although off duty (I only worked weekends and evenings) I offered to speak with him first to de-escalate the situation, before escalating it to head office. I could see the strain etched on his face. His eyes were puffy from crying, and he fidgeted nervously as he pulled out several scraps of torn paper from his pocket. The writing on them was nearly illegible, a jumble of words and phrases that made little sense. Before he could even begin to explain, tears welled up in his eyes, and he broke down crying, unable to speak.

Recognizing his distress, I quietly offered him a glass of water. He took it with trembling hands, and before taking a sip, he made the sign of the cross. That simple gesture spoke volumes to me. It was a signal, a silent plea for comfort and understanding. Without hesitation, I mirrored his gesture, also making the sign of the cross myself. I asked him softly if he was a Christian, and when he nodded, I shared that I was one too. I then offered to bless him, a small act of compassion that he graciously accepted.

This moment of shared faith seemed to calm him down, grounding him in a way that words alone could not. His breathing slowed, and the tears that had been so close to the surface began to subside. Though still emotional, he was able to compose himself enough to start sharing his story. The meeting stretched on for three hours, as I patiently listened, putting myself in his shoes, asking him both open and closed-ended questions to gently guide him through his thoughts and emotions.

Bit by bit, I was able to piece together the fragments of his story. MM's primary struggle was with his self-esteem. He interpreted almost anything anyone said to him as a put-down or a sign of suspicion, which only deepened his sense of isolation and confusion. This made it incredibly difficult for him to interact with others, especially in situations where he needed help or support.

Recognizing the depth of MM's struggle, I knew I needed to explain his situation to Sean to help him better understand the young man's needs. It was as though a light bulb switched on for Sean, and he immediately adjusted his approach, treating MM with empathy and kindness rather than frustration. Over time, as I continued to coach and mentor Sean, he gained both experience and confidence, ultimately becoming known for his ability to meet and exceed customer expectations. Sean not only came to understand MM's emotional challenges but also learned how to communicate in a way that made MM feel supported and understood, rather than judged or misunderstood.

There was a noticeable shift in MM as his relationship with Sean as his people skills improved. Although MM was still fragile, battling his demons, he developed a sense of hope, knowing that he was finally being heard and that steps were being taken to address his needs with the care and compassion he deserved as a respected long-term tenant.

MM's story reveals the power of empathy and kindness. Truly, empathy and kindness are the cornerstones of exceptional customer service. Think of a time when someone truly listened to you, made you feel understood, and responded with kindness. How did it feel? It is likely you felt valued and respected. This is the same feeling that, as customer whisperers, we seek to provide in our interactions. Cultivating empathy means putting yourself in the customer's shoes, understanding their feelings, and responding with compassion.

Kindness is expressed through small acts of consideration and support. A warm smile, a gentle tone, or a thoughtful gesture can make a significant difference in someone's day. By practicing empathy and kindness, you create a positive ripple effect that enhances the overall service experience and builds stronger connections with those you serve.

Most humans find empathy comes naturally when given the space for it to arise. But for those for whom it feels a bit more difficult to access, the practice of self-care is helpful.

Fostering a Culture of Respect

Respect is the bedrock of any healthy and productive work environment. It involves recognizing the inherent worth of every individual and treating them with dignity. Fostering a culture of respect means consistently demonstrating courteous behavior, valuing diverse perspectives, and creating an inclusive atmosphere where everyone feels appreciated.

As I continued working with Sean, who was also a Christian, he became someone with a deep well of empathy, a gentle demeanor, and a remarkable ability to connect with tenants on a personal level. He developed a reputation for not only meeting his customers' business needs but also understanding and addressing the underlying emotional challenges they faced. His newfound professional expertise made him the perfect match for MM.

When MM walked into Sean office now, an immediate sense of ease was felt in the room. Sean greeted him with a warm smile, his eyes kind and understanding, and he mirrored his action when he made the sign of the cross before speaking. He took the time to listen, truly listen, to MM's story, allowing him to express his thoughts and feelings without fear of judgment. Unlike his previous encounters, this time, MM felt understood each time he spoke with Sean. Sean's approach became patient and compassionate; it was clear he was trying to see the world through MM's eyes.

Over the course of time, as I continued to coach and mentor Sean, he not only addressed all of MM's housing needs, carefully guiding him through the steps required to resolve his issues, but he also recognized the deeper emotional struggles he was facing. Sensing his vulnerability, he offered him spiritual support, drawing on his own faith to help bolster his. He spoke to him about the importance of self-care, teaching him techniques to manage his emotions and improve his mental health. Sean introduced him to the concept of positive thinking, helping him reframe his negative thoughts and focus on the good in his life.

But Sean's support didn't end when the meetings ended. He understood that MM needed consistent reassurance and positivity to help him navigate his challenges. So, he made it a point to keep in touch with him every day, even if only for a few minutes, to offer a boost of encouragement, a blessing and positivity. These brief check-ins became a lifeline for MM, providing him with a sense of stability and hope that he had been missing for so long.

A few months after his first meeting with Sean, MM called me. His voice was filled with an excitement I had never heard before. He first asked for a blessing, a request that warmed my heart, and then went on to express how satisfied and happy he was with Sean. He told me that Sean seemed to understand his situation as if he had lived it himself. He was amazed at how he had not only met all his residential needs but had also gone above and beyond by providing him with the spiritual and emotional support he so desperately needed.

MM spoke of how Sean had taught him about the power of self-care and positive thinking, and how these teachings were already starting to make a difference in his life. He felt a renewed sense of hope and purpose, something that had been absent for so long. He was particularly grateful for the daily check-ins and blessings, which gave him the strength to face each new day with a bit more confidence and peace.

As I listened to MM, I couldn't help but feel a deep sense of satisfaction and pride in the outcome. The connection between MM and Sean had blossomed, and it was clear that Sean's influence was a transforming MM life in ways that went far beyond the call of duty. MM had found not just a perfect building manager, but an ally, a mentor, and a friend who was helping him rebuild his life, one positive step at a time.

In that moment, I realized that this was what it truly meant to serve others, to see beyond the surface, to understand the unique needs of each individual, and to provide the kind of support that could make a lasting difference. MM's story was a testament to the power of empathy, understanding, and kindness, and it reinforced my belief in the importance of matching the right people with the right support. The transformation in MM's life was profound, and it all began with a simple act of faith, a shared gesture of compassion, and a commitment to seeing him as more than just a customer, but as a person deserving of care, respect, and love.

In your day-to-day interactions with others, showing respect can be as simple as actively listening, acknowledging their contributions, and addressing people with polite and considerate language. If you have a very full cup and the wherewithal, plus the customer's permission to speak to them about spiritual themes, you might show up more like Sean. Of course, Sean is a building manager, and that is very different from the business owner, teacher, government employee or retail worker. However, you are still serving a human, in a different yet connected environment. The need for a new stereo, if you are serving customers in a retail setting, will likely not need such depth of intimacy for you to meet that customer's need. Sean's example above shows the extreme to which customer whispering can reach, in any environment. Chances are as a retail worker you may not need to access spirituality and emotions to meet the needs of your customers.

Either way, whether in a retail store, apartment complex or a government setting, empathy, kindness, and the seeking of connection with your customer are the strongest ways to show up and create a situation in which everyone wins. A respectful environment like this not only enhances morale but also promotes collaboration and trust. When respect is a fundamental part of the workplace culture, it reflects in every interaction, leading to more positive and effective service delivery.

Respect is the bedrock of any healthy and productive work environment. It involves recognizing the inherent worth of every individual and treating them with dignity. Fostering a culture of respect means consistently demonstrating courteous behavior, valuing diverse perspectives, and creating an inclusive atmosphere where everyone feels appreciated.

In our residential building, respect was more than just a word. It was a practice. It manifested in the way we spoke to one another, the way we listened, and the way we acknowledged each other's contributions. Showing respect could be as simple as actively listening during a conversation, acknowledging a tenant or colleague's hard work, or addressing someone with polite and considerate language. These small acts of respect added up, creating an environment where morale was high, collaboration flourished, and trust was a natural outcome.

By promoting respect as a fundamental part of our workplace culture, we saw it reflected in every interaction, both internally among residents and externally with customers. This emphasis on respect led to more positive and effective service delivery. When customers felt respected and valued, they were more likely to trust us, to open up about their needs, and to engage in the process of finding solutions.

Sean's success stories were a powerful reminder of the impact that respect and empathy can have. They showed us that when we take the time to truly listen, to understand, and to go that extra mile, we don't just meet expectations, we exceed them. And in doing so, we foster a work environment where everyone, from staff to customers, feels respected, valued, and supported.

Sean developed a remarkable ability to connect with his customers, consistently meeting and exceeding their expectations. From that moment on, his dedication and compassion were evident in every interaction he had. It wasn't long before his customers, like MM, began reaching out to me directly, eager to share their experiences. I received messages, voicemails, visits, and even letters, all filled with stories of how Sean had gone above and beyond his duties to serve them. These testimonials spoke of his unwavering commitment, his ability to listen, and the extra steps he took to ensure that each person felt valued and understood.

I believe in celebrating the successes of my colleagues and promoting the good work they do. Sean's consistent excellence provided the perfect opportunity to foster a culture of respect within our workplace. I encouraged him to leverage his strengths by sharing his good news stories at our quarterly building managers' meetings. These meetings became a platform where managers could not only learn from one another but also be inspired by the positive impact they were making on the lives of their customers.

In addition to sharing these stories at meetings, I also featured them in our quarterly newsletter. By highlighting Sean's and others' contributions, I aimed to create a ripple effect throughout the organization, encouraging everyone to embrace the same level of dedication and care in their work. These stories were not just about individual achievements; they were about building a workplace where respect and kindness were the cornerstones of every interaction.

Inspired by Sean's example, the culture of respect in our organization grew stronger. Colleagues began to share their own stories of going above and beyond for their customers. This collective focus on respect and excellence transformed our workplace into one where every individual's worth was recognized, and where the standard of care we provided was a reflection of our shared values.

Building on the culture of respect and excellence that Sean and others had cultivated, I began to see the tangible impact of our efforts reflected in the stories and testimonials we collected. These were not just anecdotes. They were powerful evidence of the outstanding service we consistently provided. Customers praised the empathy, understanding, and dedication they received, and it was clear that our focus on respect was making a significant difference in their lives.

Inspired by the positive feedback and the consistent excellence demonstrated, I knew that their hard work deserved broader recognition. Each year, I carefully compiled the stories, letters, and customer testimonials, highlighting the ways in which they went above and beyond to serve our customers with compassion, love and respect. With this evidence in hand, I proudly nominated Sean for Building Manager of the Year Award, which recognized his outstanding contributions to service and excellence in customer service.

This award was one of the highest honors in our organization, and competition was always fierce. However, the stories we had collected were a testament to the unique culture we had built, one where respect, empathy, and exceptional service were not just goals, but daily practices. Each nomination was crafted to showcase how Sean and others not only met the needs of our customers but exceeded them in ways that had a profound and lasting impact.

Year after year, my nominations stood out among the many submissions. The judges (head office and tenants) recognized the genuine care and dedication that shone through in every story, and they understood that our achievements were the result of a cohesive and compassionate team effort. As a result, as building managers came and went, I nominated those who displayed those qualities, and they frequently won the Building Manager of the Year Award for demonstrating excellence in customer service.

Receiving the award was more than just an acknowledgment of our hard work. It was a celebration of the values we upheld. It reinforced the importance of fostering a culture where every team member felt empowered to make a difference in the lives of those we served. The awards ceremonies became a highlight of the year, a moment where we could reflect on our successes and take pride in the impact we had made.

Winning the Building Manager of the Year Award also had a ripple effect within our organization. It inspired other buildings within the organization to adopt similar practices, to focus on respect and customer-centered service, and to recognize the power of going above and beyond in their roles. The recognition elevated not just our team but the entire organization, setting a new standard for excellence in customer service.

The consistent recognition through the Building Manager of the Year Award further strengthened our team's morale and commitment. It validated the efforts of every team member and encouraged them to continue striving for excellence. It also fostered a sense of unity and pride within the team, knowing that their work was making a real difference and was being honored at the highest levels.

In the end, the awards were not just about winning—they were about affirming the values we held dear. They were a testament to the power of respect, empathy, and dedication, and a reminder that when we focus on truly serving others, we can achieve greatness together. Each year, as we stood on the stage accepting the Customer Service Award, we knew that it was not just an individual achievement, but a collective victory that reflected the heart and soul of our team.

Maintaining a Service-Oriented Attitude

A service-oriented attitude is about prioritizing the needs of the people you serve and striving to exceed their expectations. This mindset involves being proactive, responsive, and solution focused. It's about going the extra mile to ensure that every interaction leaves a positive impression.

Think of a time when you received exceptional service—perhaps a store clerk went out of their way to help you find what you needed, or a colleague stayed late to assist with a project. These actions stem from a genuine desire to help and make a difference. By adopting a service-oriented attitude, you can create memorable experiences for your customers, building loyalty and trust.

Building Trust with Customers

Trust is the foundation of all successful relationships. It is earned through consistent, reliable, and transparent actions. Building trust with customers involves being honest, keeping promises, and showing integrity in every interaction.

A crucial aspect of building trust, which became a cornerstone of our team's success, was the commitment to never judge a customer based on their appearance or how they presented themselves. We understood that our customers came from diverse walks of life, each carrying their own unique set of experiences and challenges. In our line of work, it was essential to approach every individual with an open mind, recognizing that we did not know their full story or the struggles they might be facing. As spiritually-minded people, we were always sure to honor and celebrate the unique and diverse array of faiths and spiritual beliefs that everyone who entered the building held within themselves.

This principle of non-judgment was something I emphasized repeatedly in our team meetings and training sessions. I encouraged others to look beyond surface impressions and to engage with each customer as a person of inherent worth and dignity. By doing so, we could truly understand their needs and offer the best possible support. This approach not only helped us deliver better service but also played a significant role in fostering trust.

When tenants walked into our office, they were sometimes seeking help in moments of crisis or confusion. The last thing they needed was to feel judged or dismissed based on their appearance or demeanor. By welcoming them with respect and an open mind, we were able to create an environment where they felt safe to share their concerns and challenges. This laid the groundwork for building strong, trusting relationships.

Sean, in particular, exemplified this approach in his interactions with customers like MM. He did not allow preconceived notions to cloud his judgment and always treated each customer with the utmost respect and empathy. His ability to connect with customers on a deep level, without prejudice, was a key factor in their willingness to open up and trust him. MM, for instance, found solace in Sean's non-judgmental attitude, which allowed him to communicate more freely and to finally get the help he needed.

This culture of trust and respect extended beyond individual interactions. It became a defining feature of our team and the way we operated as a whole. We knew that by approaching every situation with an open mind and a focus on understanding rather than judging, we could build stronger, more effective relationships with our customers. This, in turn, led to better outcomes and more satisfied customers.

Trust, once established, had a transformative effect on our work. Customers who felt respected and understood were more likely to engage with us openly, to follow through on our advice, and to work collaboratively towards resolving our mutual issues. This mutual trust also made it easier for us to advocate on their behalf, knowing that we had a clear understanding of their needs and circumstances.

In fostering a culture of non-judgment, we were able to create an inclusive environment where everyone felt valued and supported. This not only enhanced our service delivery but also strengthened the bonds within our team. We became more attuned to each other's strengths and challenges, working together with a shared commitment to treating everyone—customers and colleagues alike—with the respect and understanding they deserved.

As we continued to build and reinforce trust with our customers, it became clear that this was not just a best practice but a vital part of our success. The trust we cultivated enabled us to exceed expectations, win awards, and, most importantly, make a meaningful difference in the lives of those we served. It was a reminder that in our work, trust is not given—it is earned through consistent respect, empathy, and a steadfast commitment to seeing the person behind the situation.

In some cases, you may encounter situations where you cannot provide direct assistance. In these instances, it is important to recognize that there are subtle or direct ways to guide the customer to more suitable resources. Going beyond your primary duties to provide this information shows a commitment to their well-being. Giving customers a little extra time to offer guidance and connect them to additional support can make a significant difference, ensuring they receive the help they need even if it's not directly from you.

Trust grows when customers know they can count on you to address their needs and concerns effectively. It means being accountable for your actions and following through on commitments. Trust is also built by being transparent—sharing information openly and honestly and explaining processes and decisions clearly. When customers trust you, they are more likely to be patient, understanding, and supportive, even when challenges arise.

By embracing the principles discussed in this chapter, you can transform your approach to customer service, creating positive experiences for everyone involved. Think of these as ways to generate more power in your wand, so that when you wave it, you harness the magic within to transform complaints into heartfelt compliments like the warm-hearted customer whisperer you are.

Top Three Takeaways

Develop the Right Mindset: Exceptional customer service starts with self-care and positive thinking, allowing you to approach each day with clarity and optimism.

Cultivate Empathy and Kindness: Building meaningful connections with customers begins with understanding and valuing the people you serve.

Foster Respect and Trust: A respectful and loving work culture enhances every interaction, while maintaining honesty and transparency builds trust and strengthens customer loyalty.

Chapter 4
Understanding the Complaint

"In the middle of every difficulty lies opportunity."
– Albert Einstein, Theoretical Physicist, Nobel Prize Winner

4

oving forward to 1984, another city, another organization, it was a typical busy afternoon at the residential apartment/condo complex, the background humming with activity as customers came in and out of the building. The receptionist, busy managing a steady stream of visitors, looked up to see a woman in her mid-40s entering the office. She was dressed in a modest outfit – a long skirt that flowed to her ankles and a similar tunic-style top that hung below her waist. She also wore a hijab that framed her face with grace. Her expression was calm, yet there was a noticeable tension in her eyes as she approached the reception desk. Her name was Samira.

Samira (name changed) had come to meet with the building manager as he was away when she moved in, Kunal (name changed), a newly hired building manager who was also in his mid-40s. Kunal was a practicing Sikh and as such, wore a turban and a neatly trimmed beard. As he prepared for their meeting, Kunal noticed several similarities that resonated with his own cultural background. The modesty of Samira's attire, the traditional clothing that reflected a shared value of humility, and the way she carried herself with quiet dignity reminded Kunal of the women in his own community. Her subtle but familiar accent when she spoke with the receptionist hinted at a linguistic heritage that might intersect with his own. Even the way Samira adjusted her hijab, with practiced care, was reminiscent of the way women in his family adjusted their scarves.

It was a routine appointment, and based on his review of her file, there was nothing unusual that might have hinted at what was to come. These visible commonalities led Kunal to believe they might share a cultural background, perhaps even coming from neighboring regions or the same country. He felt a sense of connection and was eager to help her, assuming their shared cultural understanding might make the interaction smoother. As Samira reached the desk and was informed that Kunal was ready to see her, a sudden change swept over her face. She looked over at Kunal, her eyes narrowing slightly as she took in his appearance. Almost immediately, Samira turned back to the receptionist, her voice firm and clear. "I don't want to meet with him," she said, her words tinged with discomfort. "I would like to see the lady who took my application." That was me. She did not realize that I was only a weekend relief building manager.

In the world of housing services, this comment was considered a "complaint." Customer complaints are par for the course, no matter from where you are serving. In my years in human services, a request like this required sensitivity, and you will learn more about how we resolved this specific incident as the chapter unfolds. In a business setting, a situation like this could easily lead to the loss of a customer if not handled well. In a for profit industry, we can't lose good customers, and it is essential that we treat them in ways that make them welcome, and this includes managing complaints with grace.

At the bottom of handling complaints with expertise, is excellence in communication. The establishment of effective communication is crucial in horse whispering, and the same goes for customer whispering. The horse and trainer must create a strong line of communication. Doing so leads to mutual understanding and more responsiveness to the signals the trainer gives the horse. Communication in this context means everything; not just your words, but your tone of voice, body language, other non-verbal cues, and then also attuning to those same non-verbal elements in the other party, too.

Horse whisperers pay close attention and listen deeply to the horse's reactions in order to better communicate with them. This is exactly what customer whisperers seek to do. When done so, a customer whisperer creates magic, which is harmony that leads to better outcomes—outcomes that matter greatly whenever a complaint is involved.

Decoding Customer Frustrations

I used to tell my colleagues, "Make every customer feel valued and heard, then wave your hand to turn their concerns into praise, like the tender customer whisperer you are." Many of them enjoyed the metaphor of being a whisperer, envisioning themselves coming to the aid of the wild horses who were the people we served.

Understanding a customer's frustration is akin to deciphering a complex puzzle. When a customer approaches you with a complaint, it's easy to get caught up in the details of their issue. However, the true art lies in recognizing the underlying emotions driving their dissatisfaction. Think of it like peeling an onion, with each layer you uncover, you get closer to the core of their concern. By asking thoughtful questions and genuinely listening, you can slowly start to decode the frustration, eventually accessing the root cause.

At Samira's request, I knew I had to approach this situation with care, peeling back the layers of her frustration to get to the heart of the matter.

After Samira requested to speak with a female, Kunal called me and asked me if I would speak with her. A glance at Samira's file revealed no specific reasons for this request. Understanding the request, but aware that on a Friday afternoon at 3 pm, I would not be on duty Kunal informed Samira that it would be the next day before the female building manager would be available to meet with her.

This answer did not sit well with Samira. Her posture stiffened, and a trace of frustration appeared on her face. "I don't believe you," she said, her tone firm, indicating a growing mistrust. "I need to speak with someone who has more authority than you," she told Kumal.

Kumal, recognizing Samira's determination, and sensing the importance of the situation, approached Samira in the waiting area, intending to explain the staffing situation and offer her some reassurance.

However, as soon as Samira saw him approaching, she quickly shook her head. "I'm sorry, I won't speak with you," she repeated, her voice carrying a note of finality. Kunal paused, respecting her request. After a brief moment, he agreed to call me at home again, and I agreed to speak with Samira.

The receptionist escorted Samira to an interview room, providing her with some privacy, and placed the call to me. I answered promptly. As soon as I heard the details, I became aware that this situation required a delicate touch. As Samira took the call, I could sense her unease even through the phone. She greeted me politely but with a guarded tone, clearly unsettled by the events that had unfolded.

I began by asking thoughtful questions, not only to understand her immediate concern but also to uncover the deeper reasons behind her refusal to meet with a male caseworker. "I understand that this situation has been difficult for you," I said gently. "Can you tell me more about why you feel uncomfortable speaking with the male building manager today?"

Samira hesitated for a moment, and then her voice softened slightly. "It's not about him personally," she began, choosing her words carefully. "But in my culture, there are certain things I don't feel comfortable discussing with a man. Women understand my situation without me having to explain too much."

As she spoke, I could hear the layers of her concern beginning to unfold. It wasn't just about the specific issue at hand. It was about her need to feel understood and respected within the context of her cultural and personal boundaries. Her request was rooted in a deep-seated discomfort, one that was tied to her cultural upbringing and life experience.

"I completely understand where you're coming from," I replied, acknowledging her feelings. "Your comfort and trust are very important to us. I'm sorry that we weren't able to accommodate your request immediately, but I assure you that we're here to support you in a way that makes you feel respected and understood."

With that, I offered to personally oversee the matter to ensure her concerns were addressed promptly, adding a note in her file the next day, to ensure she wouldn't have to make the same request each time. Before interacting with new residents, building managers review their files to alert them of the customer's situation. This process not only ensures that Samira's needs are consistently met but also highlights the importance of recognizing and respecting cultural differences in service delivery. This approach helped to calm her, and while she still had to wait a short while, knowing that her needs were being taken seriously made a significant difference in her willingness to cooperate.

As the conversation ended, the tension that had initially marked Samira's voice had eased, replaced by a sense of relief. She thanked me for understanding her situation and for taking the time to listen without judgment. It was clear that by addressing not just the logistical issue but also the emotional layers of her complaint, I had helped restore her trust in our service.

This experience reinforced the importance of truly listening to our customers, understanding their perspectives, and responding with empathy and respect. In doing so, we not only resolve their immediate concerns but also build a foundation of trust that can carry through in future interactions.

Seeing the Bigger Picture

When faced with a complaint, it's essential we strive to see the bigger picture. Often, a single complaint can reveal larger systemic issues within your service or product. Imagine a leaky faucet in a house. While it's a minor annoyance, it could indicate deeper plumbing issues that need attention. Similarly, customer complaints can serve as valuable feedback, highlighting areas that require improvement. By stepping back and examining the broader context, you can identify patterns and implement changes that benefit all customers.

As I continued my conversation with Samira, I realized that the situation expanded beyond more than just a single interaction. This was an opportunity to see the bigger picture. Samira's discomfort with meeting a man was not just an isolated incident. It could be indicative of a larger, systemic issue within our service delivery, specifically the level of cultural awareness and sensitivity of our colleagues. I knew that if this customer had concerns about speaking to a man, there might be others who felt similarly but had not voiced their concerns openly.

I knew I had to get to the bigger picture surrounding this complaint. I made a mental note to discuss this situation with the building manager, not just to address this particular customer's needs, but to consider how we could better serve other customers in similar circumstances. Perhaps we needed to review our processes or ensure that customers felt empowered to make a request they were comfortable with from the outset.

By stepping back and examining the broader context, I could see that this complaint was a valuable piece of feedback. It highlighted the importance of cultural sensitivity and the need for flexibility in our service delivery. Understanding this allowed me to approach the situation not just as a problem to be solved, but as an opportunity to improve our overall service.

Understanding these cultural nuances is crucial in providing exceptional customer service. It helps organizations like ours and others to better serve diverse communities by being attuned to subtle cues and specific needs. By fostering awareness and sensitivity to different cultural practices, we can create a more inclusive environment that respects and accommodates everyone's unique requirements.

Why People Complain

People complain for various reasons, often due to unmet expectations or frustration. It is important to understand what customers expect before they interact with you or your organization. They want to feel welcome, be treated with courtesy, and engage with knowledgeable staff about the services or products offered. By understanding these expectations, you can consistently deliver excellent service. Complaints act as signals, pointing out areas that need attention. Just like a fire alarm warns of danger, customer complaints highlight issues that require resolution. Addressing the root causes leads to more effective solutions and happier customers.

Finding the Hidden Opportunity

Every complaint is an opportunity in disguise. When a customer brings an issue to your attention, they're giving you a chance to make things right and to improve your service. Consider a complaint as a diamond in the rough. With the right approach, you can turn it into a shining gem. By addressing complaints effectively, you not only resolve the immediate issue but also demonstrate your commitment to customer satisfaction, potentially turning a dissatisfied customer into a loyal advocate.

For Samira, by bringing her issue to our attention, she was giving us the opportunity to make things right. I recognized that addressing her concerns effectively could not only resolve the immediate issue but also demonstrate our commitment to her satisfaction, ensuring that she would be a happy long-term tenant. If we handled this well, there was a strong possibility that we could turn a dissatisfied customer into a loyal advocate. Even better, we could help other women with a similar cultural background to Samira, with more knowledge, awareness and preparation.

As I spoke with Samira, I made sure to keep my tone positive and constructive. I acknowledged her feelings and assured her that we were committed to finding a solution that respected her needs. This wasn't just about fixing a problem. It was about building a bridge through every interaction. Each conversation, each decision, was an opportunity to strengthen our relationship with her and, by extension, with all our customers.

Building Bridges Through Every Interaction

Each interaction with a customer is an opportunity to build a bridge. Whether the interaction is positive or negative, your response shapes the relationship. Picture a bridge being constructed one plank at a time. Each positive interaction adds a plank, strengthening the connection. Even when dealing with complaints, maintaining a positive and constructive attitude can transform the interaction from a potential confrontation into a collaborative problem-solving session. This approach not only resolves the issue at hand but also reinforces the customer's trust in your service.

In the days that followed, my moment with Samira in which I built a bridge and formed a relationship, I shared the experience with Kunal, emphasizing the lessons we had learned. We discussed the importance of seeing the bigger picture when handling complaints, finding hidden opportunities in every issue, and building bridges through every interaction. We also explored ways to create unforgettable experiences for our customers, ensuring that every touchpoint left them feeling valued and respected.

The incident with Samira became a catalyst for positive change within our organization, prompting us to offer more flexible service options. Whenever a customer requested a different person, I took the opportunity to gently explore the reasons behind it, understanding what was working and what wasn't, to find the best fit. While customers cannot directly choose those who serve them, this approach helped us to retain them as customers by better meeting their needs

The organization ensured that staff received cultural sensitivity training, soliciting strong educators on the topic to do staff workshops and trainings. We also made follow-up calls, a standard practice, recognizing the value they added to the customer experience.

In the end, Samira's complaint did more than highlight a service gap. It helped us improve our approach, build stronger relationships with our customers, the residents, and reinforce our commitment to providing exceptional, respectful service. It was a powerful reminder that every challenge presents an opportunity to grow, and that by focusing on the bigger picture, we can create meaningful, lasting change.

The Power of a Warm Welcome

First impressions matter, and a warm welcome sets the tone for the entire customer experience. Imagine walking into a store and being greeted with a genuine smile and a friendly hello. This simple act can immediately put you at ease and make you feel valued. In the context of customer complaints, a warm and empathetic greeting can defuse tension and create a more positive environment for resolving issues. It shows the customer that you're approachable and ready to help, paving the way for a constructive dialogue.

As we implemented the changes inspired by Samira's complaint, I couldn't help but reflect on the power of a warm welcome in shaping the customer experience. Knowing just how much first impressions truly matter, it follows that a warm, empathetic greeting sets the tone for everything that comes after that initial exchange. I made it a point to remind my team that when a customer walks through our doors, whether they are calm or distressed, our first interaction should be one of genuine care and friendliness. This simple act of welcoming someone with a smile and a sincere hello can immediately put them at ease, signaling that they are valued and that we are here to help.

For bonuses go to ...

When Samira came into our office that day, the tension was palpable. By treating her with respect and offering a warm, understanding approach, we were able to defuse much of that tension. This approach became even more important as we continued to deal with other customers who were difficult to serve. Handling difficult situations is one of the most challenging aspects of customer service. Some customers arrive frustrated, angry, or even on the verge of a breakdown. It's essential to remain calm and composed, listening actively to their concerns without interrupting, and acknowledging their frustrations with empathy.

During my conversation with Samira, I kept this in mind. I listened carefully, responded calmly, and made sure she knew that her feelings were valid. This approach helped to de-escalate the situation, allowing us to move toward a resolution. But I also knew that there would be times when a situation might become unmanageable. It's crucial to have protocols in place for such scenarios, ensuring that we can call on more senior managers, healthcare providers, or even law enforcement if necessary to keep everyone safe.

In this case, involving a female manager, myself, though remotely initially, was the right move. By taking the time to listen to Samira, understand her needs and eventually cultural influences, and offer an appropriate solution, we were able to redirect her to the right resource and provide the support she needed. This experience reinforced the importance of being prepared to guide customers to the right support, even when the solution isn't immediately apparent.

Creating Unforgettable Experiences

Memorable customer service experiences are created through attention to detail and a personal touch. Think of a time when you received exceptional service that left a lasting impression. Perhaps it was a handwritten thank-you note or an unexpected follow-up call. These small gestures show customers that you care and are willing to go the extra mile.

I knew I wanted to create an unforgettable experience for Samira, so I arranged for a follow-up meeting with her, ensuring that Samira would receive the care and attention she deserved. But I didn't stop there. I made a point of personally following up with her after the meeting. A few days later, I called Samira to check in, not just to see if her immediate needs had been met, but to ask how she was feeling and if there was anything more, we could do for her.

This unexpected follow-up was a small gesture, but it made a significant impact. Samira expressed her appreciation for the extra care and attention, and it was clear that her trust in our service had been restored. By taking that extra step, I was able to turn a potentially negative experience into a positive one, leaving her with a lasting impression of our commitment to her well-being.

Creating such unforgettable experiences requires attention to detail and a personal touch. By consistently making these efforts, we build a reputation for excellence and foster long-term customer loyalty.

Dealing with Difficult to Serve Customers

In 1990, 88-year-old Mr. Davis, a World War 1 veteran, was upset about a delay in his at home personal care, suggesting that the system was against him. As his weekend personal support worker (PSW), I was delayed in getting to his home by 7 a.m. due to a snowstorm which left the city incapacitated for many hours. His frustration turned to anger, and he demanded immediate attention. Mr. Davis expressed his anger aggressively. He was shouting that he was hungry and could be heard over the phone, pounding on the table with his fist. I remained calm, allowing him to vent without interruption, and showed him that I was genuinely listening to his concerns.

Despite my efforts, Mr. Davis remained on edge, doubting that anyone could help him. To de-escalate the situation, I used calming techniques,

73

maintained a composed tone, gave him my full attention, and used open communication language to convey my willingness to help. I gently redirected the conversation toward resolving his issue, asking clarifying questions to show I was truly listening. I understood that he was hungry and was looking for food. I directed him to his kitchen cupboard where I had placed some dried goods after shopping for him the previous week. I guided him step by step to prepare a simple breakfast of cereal and milk.

Understanding that the PSW manager in the local care office was busy with similar situations, I knew I needed to resolve the issue myself. I reassured Mr. Davis that I would personally oversee his case to ensure a resolution. By reinforcing my commitment to finding a solution, I gradually helped him to calm down, staying with him on the phone and letting him know that I would come to his home as soon as my road was plowed.

Although still frustrated, he had a clearer understanding of the next steps and a sense that his concerns were taken seriously. I left the agency a message with my plan and to see if there was another PSW living closer to him to him who could look in on him just to reassure him. I also asked him if he had the contact information of any of his neighbors, to which he responded that he did. He gave me the number, and I called the neighbor, introducing myself and the situation and asked him if he was able to check in on Mr. Davis.

While I was still on the phone with him, he said there was a knock on his door. The neighbor traveling by snow machine was checking up on him to make sure he was OK. This instantly alleviated all his concerns, as the man promised to check in on him again during the day. By 9 a.m. two hours later, as soon as the roads were cleared, I visited him and consoled him and took the opportunity to show him some simple things he could do if the situation arose again. He was very happy to see me and apologized for his frustration. I assured him, that his well-being was my utmost concern and that I cared deeply about his safety. He gave me a hug and thanked me for being there for him by phone, for sending someone to check on him and for coming as soon as I could. He understood that snowstorms have the capacity to cripple a city and remembered back to when he was a child, and the roads did not get ploughed sometimes for a whole week after a heavy snow fall. He asked my forgiveness, and I assured him that I understood and did not take his comments personally. I took control to resolve the issues directly and used available organizational resources to provide temporary relief.

Here are three strong tips for managing a difficult customer:

Active Listening: Allow the customer to express their frustrations without interruption. Actively listening shows that you genuinely care about their concerns, which can help to de-escalate the situation and make the customer feel heard and validated.

Stay Calm and Empathetic: Maintain a calm and steady tone while acknowledging the customer's frustration. Showing empathy helps to defuse tension and build rapport, even when faced with aggressive behavior.

Take Control and Resolve Issues Directly: If the situation remains tense, confidently take control by focusing on finding a solution yourself. Reassure the customer that you are committed to resolving their issue, which can help to calm them down and restore their confidence in the service they are receiving.

Self-Care and Not Taking It Personally

Dealing with difficult customers can be emotionally taxing, but it's important not to take it personally. Not taking things personally can be an exceptional challenge to many people, yet there is great freedom in this practice once you understand the value. By not taking things personally, you can then understand that their frustration is directed at the situation, not at you as an individual.

Self-care is also a powerful ally when it comes to dealing with difficult customers. After handling a challenging interaction, it is helpful (sometimes essential) that you take some time to recoup and recharge. This could involve deep breathing exercises, talking to a trusted colleague, or debriefing the situation with your manager to pull out the lessons and opportunities it provided. Other strategies might include going for a walk, meditating, or even allowing yourself to cry if needed.

Utilize any organizational resources available, such as temporary assistance strategies, which can offer support and counseling. Consulting a health care professional may also be beneficial if stress becomes overwhelming. I cannot emphasize enough how crucial self-care is in maintaining your well-being and ensuring you can continue to serve other customers effectively. Remember, taking care of yourself enables you to provide the best possible service to others.

As much as I focused on helping Samira, and on improving our service, I also had to remind myself and my team not to take these difficult interactions personally. It's easy to feel hurt or overwhelmed when a customer's frustration is directed at you, but again, it's important to remember that their anger is often a response to the situation, not to you as an individual. Whenever I experienced particularly challenging interactions, I always made it a priority to take time for self-care. I encouraged my team to do the same, whether that meant taking a few deep breaths, stepping outside for fresh air, or talking through the situation with a trusted colleague.

Utilizing organizational resources, such as our employee assistance program, also became an essential part of our self-care routine. Knowing that we had access to support and counseling if the stress became too much was a comfort.

Self-care isn't just about maintaining our well-being. It's about ensuring we can continue to serve our customers with the compassion and empathy they deserve. By taking care of ourselves, we are better equipped to handle the next challenging situation that comes our way, and we can continue to build the trust and respect that form the foundation of our work.

As the weeks passed after our incident with Samira, the changes we made began to bear fruit. Customers felt more comfortable and respected, and our staff felt more confident in their ability to handle difficult situations. Samira became a symbol of our commitment to listening, understanding, and adapting our services to meet the diverse needs of our customers.

In the end, what started as a challenging situation transformed into an opportunity for growth and improvement. We had not only resolved Samira's issue but also made lasting changes that benefited everyone who walked through our doors. Through the power of a warm welcome, the skill of dealing with difficult customers, and the importance of self-care, we created an environment where trust, respect, and excellent service were the cornerstones of our success.

Each time we successfully navigated a challenging interaction, it reinforced the belief that every complaint is an opportunity to build a bridge and create an unforgettable experience. By staying committed to these principles, we continued to foster a culture of excellence and trust that would serve us well in the years to come.

Top Three Takeaways

Your wand is your heart. As you wave your wand, you are using your heart and turning complaints into compliments, like the true, kind-hearted customer whisperer you are.

Always provide a warm welcome at the start of every customer interaction, using kindness and empathy to create positive experiences.

Look beyond surface-level complaints to uncover deeper insights and hidden opportunities, transforming them into valuable feedback.

Approach difficult customers with empathy, focusing on their needs without taking it personally, and seek additional support when necessary to ensure the best outcome.

Chapter 5
Crafting the Perfect Response

*"Kind words can be short and easy to speak,
but their echoes are truly endless."*
– Mother Teresa, Nobel Peace Prize Winner

5

I n the previous chapter, Samira's story showed one way of crafting the perfect response to a customer complaint. It is truly by responding with compassion that we wave our wands, transforming a complaint into an appreciation. This is the art of being a charming customer whisperer.

A good horse whisperer understands innately that they need to act from a place of grounded strength, with the key word in this sentence being "act." If a horse whisperer loses their footing and begins reacting to the horse, the horse will not benefit. The art of horse whispering relies upon great awareness in the trainer and the ability to set and hold a safe container for the horse to express and learn within. In that container, the trainer is the leader. Excellent leaders strive to act, not react. For a horse whisperer, reacting without thinking in an interaction could prove harmful for both horse and trainer. Presence is essential, because we can only act when we come from a place of full present awareness.

Of course, humans are constantly engaging in a dance of act-react. In the modern, internet-influenced world, we are encouraged to react even more. Consider how often you've seen a YouTube video that shows a person reacting to another video they have seen. Given the fact that so much social media thrives on people's tendency to react, and specifically react with biased outrage, it is easy to feel concerned that we may have tilted out of balance on the topic. Many people are unaware as to how often they are truly acting, versus reacting.

When it comes to customer complaints, whether you act or react is the difference between being a customer service provider and a true customer whisperer. Because a customer service provider who does not really care about anything beyond the paycheck is more likely to meet a customer's complaint – their reaction to the service or product – with the same energy the customer is bringing to the situation. But we cannot fight fire with fire; the customer whisperer is the one who acts in the moment, not reacts to the customer complaint.

As a horse trainer will seek to be proactive and work with the horse in that way to provide a safe experience for all, so will a good customer whisperer do the same. This is how customer complaints get resolved effectively, and is one of the keys to crafting the perfect response.

A Team Effort

Crafting the right response to a complaint sometimes involves both individual actions and organizational systems to reduce future issues. Each complaint is unique, but the best responses often come from collaboration at different levels within an organization or system.

The COVID-19 pandemic took the world by surprise and unfolded extremely rapidly. The media reported how the World Health used previous research to guide countries on actions to take. As a result, Ontario declared a state of emergency. At the start of the pandemic lockdown in Canada, government offices were temporarily closed as they worked to develop safe return-to-work protocols. Customers, who were used to in-person meetings, suddenly had to adjust to communicating by phone, which was a big change for many. To address this, government employees were provided with a cell phone and laptop, allowing them to access a virtual platform that enhanced communication with both customers and colleagues. Instead of being handed over in person, documents could now be conveniently uploaded to government portals for streamlined processing.

In some essential service organizations small teams went into closed offices daily to process documents that were placed in after-hours mail slots. Faxes were also retrieved electronically in an email format, allowing operations to continue smoothly despite the office closure.

However, these adjustments were not without their difficulties. Many customers, especially those without access to a phone or computer, found this new system challenging. The digital divide became more apparent than ever, as some customers struggled to adapt to these new methods of communication, and others did not even have the devices necessary to use these new methods of communication, or if they somehow had the device, they did not always have WIFI. It was clear that while the system worked for many, there were still gaps that needed to be addressed to ensure that every customer had access to the support they needed.

During this challenging period, all levels of governments faced an overwhelming number of complaints from customers and community organizations who were struggling to survive. The phone lines were inundated with calls, and staff were stretched thin, trying to manage the influx while also processing necessary paperwork. It was clear that the situation was escalating. What was a customer service concern was veering towards a labor relations concern, too.

In an ordinary business setting, the volume of complaints would never be as high as that which were received during this period. It is rare for a corporation to overhaul their services in response to customer complaints, yet that is precisely what the Canadian and Ontario governments did during this crisis.

In contrast, businesses across various industries faced similar challenges but approached their responses and messaging about the pandemic in diverse ways. Some companies, like many not-for-profit agencies, particularly those in the health care and essential services sectors, acted swiftly, prioritizing transparency with frequent communication to reassure their customers and employees. They emphasized safety protocols, provided and adapted their services to meet the rapidly changing demands. Meanwhile, some business struggled to keep pace with the evolving situation, resulting in inconsistent messaging and delayed responses that sometimes eroded customer trust. The variety in responses highlighted the importance of a well-coordinated, proactive approach, one that anticipates potential issues, adapts swiftly to new challenges, and maintains clear and consistent communication to uphold trust and confidence during a crisis.

Recognizing the urgency of the pandemic, government executives stepped in with decisive action. To alleviate the pressure and address the immediate needs of customers, the ministry made the proactive decision to automatically extend benefits that were about to expire and to lift holds or suspensions without requiring the usual supporting documentation. This move was crucial in preventing customers from falling through the cracks during this unprecedented time. Carefully constructed letters with the rights words were promptly sent to all affected customers, informing them of these changes and providing reassurance that their benefits would continue uninterrupted, transforming a tense situation into a positive experience.

For customers receiving payments through direct deposit, or debit cards, the transition was smooth and seamless. Their benefits were delivered without any disruption, offering them some relief during an already stressful period. The governments also ensured that clear and accessible communication was a priority. The general office lines and all staff phone messages were updated with bilingual information, explaining the changes. Additionally, signs with this information were posted on all doors and windows in both English and French, ensuring that everyone had access to the guidance they needed. Crafting the perfect response using kind and thoughtful language turned tense situations into positive experiences. The volume of calls reduced significantly, and staff could take the time to personalize and tailor their communication to fit each customer's unique needs and circumstances. While setting up this new system, the governments worked together and paid special attention to its most vulnerable customers. The media broadcasted that the Federal

Government introduced The Canada Emergency Response Benefit (CERB) providing financial support to employed and self-employed Canadians who were directly affected by COVID-19.

Governments and public health authorities across Canada continued to adjust their public health advice based on their local situations. The Ontario government, following the protocols established by the Public Health started preparing to open its office to serve its most vulnerable customers. In preparation for this reopening, the Ontario Government took extensive precautions to ensure a safe environment for both staff and customers. Staff members were provided with personal protective equipment, including masks, gloves, face shields, and Plexi-glass barriers, to reduce exposure risk. Office layouts were reconfigured for safe distancing, with floor markers indicating where customers should stand.

Hand-sanitizing stations were set up at the entrance and throughout each office, and clear signs were prominently posted on doors, windows, and walls, to explain the new safety protocols. To control the flow of customers and prevent overcrowding, a staggered schedule was implemented, limiting the number of people inside at one time. Security personnel were present to enforce these protocols and ensure safety.

An essential part of these safety measures included health screenings for both staff and customers before they were allowed entry. Screenings involved questions about recent symptoms such as fever or cough and whether they had traveled outside the country in the past 14 days. Only those who passed the screening were permitted to enter the office.

When the day arrived for the office to reopen, this commitment to warmth and empathy was evident in every interaction. Customers arrived at their designated times, were greeted warmly by staff, and were guided through the process of collecting their checks or debit cards. The ministry phone was available for them to activate their new debit cards, and throughout the day, the staff maintained a calm and supportive demeanor. Despite the challenging conditions, they ensured that every customer was treated with dignity and respect, reinforcing the ministry's dedication to providing a positive and caring service experience. Maintaining a calm, respectful, gentle, and genuinely authentic tone, fostered trust and paved the way for constructive dialogue.

These efforts had an immediate and positive impact, evidenced by a significant reduction in the volume of complaints. By extending benefits, providing clear and accessible communication, and making special accommodations for the most vulnerable, the ministry demonstrated that they were listening to their customers and responding with warmth, empathy, and respect.

Through these actions, the ministry not only addressed the immediate concerns but also reinforced the trust and respect that make up the foundation of effective public service. Even in the face of unprecedented challenges, the ministry ensured that their customers felt valued, supported, and heard. The proactive steps taken during this time showed a deep commitment to meeting the needs of all customers, particularly those most at risk, and provided a model for how to handle crises with compassion and efficiency.

In another situation with a different organization, Marsha's story highlights the impact of consistent messaging, compassionate support, and collaboration in resolving customer concerns. At age 60, Marsha began receiving Canada Pension Plan (CPP) benefits and mistakenly believed they would cover her medical expenses. When her request for medical coverage was denied, she filed several appeals and even contacted her Member of Parliament and the Ombudsman's office. However, the response was always the same: CPP does not cover medical expenses, and she was advised to consult her doctor.

Marsha assumed that this consistent messaging reflected the diligent collaboration between the CPP agent, the appeals team, the Member of Parliament, and the Ombudsman's office. Together, they ensured that everyone Marsha contacted reinforced the same advice to seek proper medical guidance. Feeling overwhelmed and unsure how to explain her situation,

Marsha turned to me, her neighbor, for help. She was particularly worried about an expensive herbal supplement she had been taking to combat tiredness, which was not covered by the Ontario Drug Benefit program. When I asked why she hadn't consulted her doctor as recommended, she admitted she didn't know how to approach the conversation and asked if I would accompany her. I agreed.

I joined Marsha at her doctor's appointment and helped her explain her situation. Fortunately, after conducting blood tests, the doctor identified an underlying illness that required specialized treatment and medication. The prescribed treatment was covered by the Ontario Drug Benefit program. This resolution was made possible by the collaborative efforts of the CPP agent, the appeals team, Member of Parliament, and the Ombudsman, whose consistent and empathetic communication guided Marsha through the process.

Marsha's experience illustrates the power of a well-crafted, compassionate response, supported by teamwork, in guiding individuals through complex situations. By transforming complaints into opportunities for understanding and resolution, the team turned Marsha's frustration into satisfaction, leaving her feeling heard, valued, and cared for.

In conclusion, the proactive steps taken during the COVID-19 pandemic, combined with the teamwork and collaboration evident in Marsha's case, demonstrate the importance of crafting the perfect response through a team effort. Whether addressing a global challenge or an individual complaint, ensuring warmth, empathy, and compassion in every interaction is key to transforming complaints into compliments and maintaining trust in public service.

For bonuses go to ...

Words that Heal

The story above demonstrates how an organization can rally together to completely overhaul services proactively to avoid or manage complaints effectively. What did we do? We did three key things. We used words that heal, we took care to communicate in a tone that was kind and empathetic, and we continued building relationships even when our "normal" way of doing so was reinterpreted to meet the needs of the circumstances surrounding us.

The right words can transform a tense situation into a positive experience. Think of words as tools. Just as a skilled carpenter uses the right tools to create a masterpiece, you can use kind and thoughtful words to repair and build relationships. When a customer is upset, responding with empathy and understanding can defuse their anger and start the healing process. Simple phrases like, "I understand how you feel," "Let's find a solution together," or "How may I assist you?" can make a significant difference in how the customer perceives the interaction. It is often more effective when customers articulate their needs before solutions are proposed.

One day, a customer came to the building manager's office in a panic on the last day of the month, because she was not going to be able to pay her rent on time, due to a missed social assistance payment. It was a Friday before a long weekend, and the anxiety in their voice made it clear this was more than just a financial issue; it was a deep fear about their immediate well-being. I paused to center myself, knowing my response could either heighten their fears or begin to ease them.

As the building manager, I calmly reassured them, acknowledging how stressful the situation must be and assuring them I would help resolve it as quickly as possible. As we spoke, I learned that the missed payment was due to the customer closing their bank account because of unauthorized withdrawals. With no active account, their payment had been held up.

I explained that this was a common issue and that there was a straightforward process to fix it. We initiated a three-way communication with the bank to confirm the account closure. Once confirmed, that the payment was canceled, she called her caseworker who also confirmed that the payment was cancelled and issued her a debit card instead, ensuring the customer had access to their funds in time for the weekend, with no disruption to paying rent or buying food.

I used words like "we'll find a solution together" and "you're not alone in this" deliberately, making every effort to convey empathy and partnership. I assured them that this was something we could fix. I took the time to explain the next steps clearly, offering reassurance at every turn, and I made it clear that their well-being was my top priority.

I believe that words have the power to heal because they can transform a moment of crisis into one of connection and trust. When we respond to complaints with compassion and understanding, we initiate a healing process. This interaction between complaint and response is not just about resolving an issue. It is about restoring a sense of safety, dignity, and respect to the individual. The healing process begins when we acknowledge the person's pain and use our words to guide them toward a place of calm and resolution.

Tone Matters

The tone of your voice is as important as the words you choose. Imagine receiving a message in a cheerful, friendly tone versus a cold, indifferent one. The same words can have entirely different effects depending on how they're delivered.

In customer service, maintaining a calm, respectful, gentle, and genuinely authentic tone, even in challenging situations, helps reassure the customer that you are there to help. Customers can sense when we are not real, and they appreciate authenticity. It's also crucial to remember that customers are not interested in hearing about our problems. The focus should always remain on them and their needs. It's like music. The melody can change the entire mood of the song.

In the human services industry, when managing written communication during a transition, such as the shift from in-person to phone, responding to letters, and signs that took place during the lockdown, it's essential to convey empathy, respect, and support. Here are some key recommendations aligned with these principles.

Start communications with warm greetings like "Dear [Name]" and end with a complimentary closing like "Best regards" to set a positive tone. Be sincere and authentic in addressing concerns, ensuring the recipient feels genuinely cared for.

Avoid using all caps, which can come across as harsh, and instead use italics or bold for emphasis. Replace demanding phrases like "Failure to comply" with more supportive language, such as "Let us know how we can assist you."

When giving instructions, be clear yet respectful. For example, instead of "Submit the required documents by [date]," try "Please submit the required documents by [date], and let us know if you need assistance."

Address complaints with empathy by acknowledging frustration and offering a sincere commitment to resolving the issue. Use inclusive language that respects diverse audiences, and avoid alarming phrases when urgency is needed.

By carefully choosing words and reviewing tone, even formal letters can convey compassion and respect, helping maintain strong customer connections while upholding effective, customer-centric communication.

Personalizing Your Approach

Each customer is unique and so should be your response. Think of it like tailoring a suit. A one-size-fits-all approach rarely works as well as something customized to fit perfectly. By personalizing your responses, you show the customer that you see them as an individual, not just another case number. Use their name, reference past interactions, and address their specific concerns directly. This personal touch can turn a standard response into a memorable, positive experience.

Personalization means knowing your clients intimately, so they don't have to repeat their stories every time they call. During the pandemic, when face-to-face interaction was no longer possible, we faced the challenge of maintaining this personalized approach while the systems were shifting. It was a difficult time, as the usual warmth and empathy that came so naturally in person had to be conveyed through screens, phones, and letters. However, we were determined not to let the distance create a disconnect.

To personalize our approach, we made it a priority to use customers' names in all communications, reference their previous interactions with us, and directly address their specific concerns. For example, when the customer above was anxious about a delayed payment, I took the time to listen to their concerns, assist them in making calls to rectify the situation. This small act of personalization helped reassure them that they were a valued individual.

During the pandemic, it wasn't easy. The lack of face-to-face interaction made it challenging to read emotions and body language, which are critical in tailoring responses. We had to rely more heavily on active listening and thoughtful word choice to convey the same level of care and attention. To overcome this, we implemented regular team check-ins to share best practices and successful strategies for maintaining personalization in our communications. This collaborative effort helped us stay connected with each other, even from a distance.

For those in business, this experience underscores an essential truth. Personalization is key to building lasting relationships, especially in challenging times. Whether you're in government or business, the principle remains the same. Flexibility and a commitment to seeing each customer as an individual can make all the difference. Personalizing your approach is like waving your wand to turn complaints into compliments. Embracing flexibility and adapting to each situation can lead to more effective and satisfactory outcomes. This personalized approach shows customers that you are attentive to their unique needs and willing to find the best solution for them, even in the most difficult circumstances.

Building Relationships Through Every Interaction

Every interaction with a customer is an opportunity to build a relationship. Whether the interaction is positive or negative, your response shapes the relationship. Picture a relationship being constructed one step at a time. Each positive interaction strengthens the connection. Even when dealing with complaints, maintaining a positive and constructive attitude can transform the interaction from a potential confrontation into a collaborative problem-solving session. This approach not only resolves the issue at hand but also reinforces the customer's trust in your service.

During the pandemic, when the human services industry shifted its systems away from in-person interactions to phone and mail-based services, employees understood the importance of maintaining a strong connection with customers. Without the face-to-face interactions that naturally built rapport, they had to find new ways to ensure customers still felt supported and heard.

One key strategy was to increase the frequency of proactive phone calls to customers. Rather than waiting for complaints to arise, employees reached out to check in, especially with those who might struggle without in-person contact. These calls were not just about delivering information; they were about listening attentively, addressing concerns immediately, and offering a personal touch to demonstrate genuine care and support.

For example, I once had a customer who lived alone and often felt depressed due to a lack of contact with others. Instead of waiting for her to reach out in frustration, I took the initiative to call her. During our brief conversation, I listened, checked in on her well-being, and offered help with any challenges she might be facing. This proactive approach turned a potential complaint into an opportunity to build trust and show genuine care for her needs.

Another way I fostered relationships was by personalizing letters and mailouts. Each communication used the customer's name, referenced past interactions, and included direct phone numbers for easy contact. These letters were thoughtfully crafted with empathy and respect, ensuring that even in written form, customers felt valued and understood.

Handling individual complaints was another critical area where we focused on relationship building. Each complaint was seen not just as an issue to be resolved but as a chance to strengthen the relationship with the customer. By embracing the power of positivity in every interaction, we waved our magical wand and acted like attentive customer whisperers. For instance, when a customer called with a concern, instead of simply addressing the issue, we took the time to explain the process, offer additional support, and follow up to ensure their satisfaction. This approach transformed a potentially negative experience into a positive one, reinforcing the customer's trust in our service.

Crafting the perfect response is essential to calming a customer complaint. But it can also be a way of behaving proactively and setting up a company or service organization's systems so that they can pre-empt complaints altogether, as the government sought to do during the pandemic.

For bonuses go to ...

By embracing the power of positivity in every customer interaction, you wave your magical wand and act like an attentive customer whisperer. Then, like a good horse whisperer, you create a container of safety and care, in which you can act, not react, with grace, building strong, lasting relationships one interaction at a time.

Top Three Takeaways

Crafting the perfect response delves into the transformative power of words and tone in customer service.

Use kind and thoughtful language to turn tense situations into positive experiences, focusing on empathy and understanding to defuse anger.

Maintain a calm, respectful, and authentic tone in all interactions, as tone plays a crucial role in navigating challenging situations.

Personalize responses to ensure individuals feel seen and valued, avoiding a one-size-fits-all approach.

Chapter 6
Empathy and Effective
Communication Superpowers

"Empathy is about finding echoes of another person in yourself."
– Mohsin Hamid, "The Reluctant Fundamentalist"

The biggest difference between horse whisperers and customer whisperers may come down to empathy. A horse whisperer can be the most empathetic human around, but the truth remains that humans can never truly understand how it feels to be a horse. When it comes to empathy, humans encourage one another to try to "walk in the shoes" of the person we want to feel empathy for. How can we do this with animals?

Despite this one challenge, horse whisperers still often display tremendous empathy as they train their horses. They also make sure to communicate effectively, and across all communication channels, from verbal to non-verbal, with attention to tone of voice, mannerisms, and body language.

The emotional state of the horse trainer is essential to the success of the training. Just as emotional states can be transferred between individuals, so can they transfer between horse and human. This is why good horse whisperers ensure they are always calm and relaxed before entering the training ring so they can promote this relaxation to the horse, which then increases trust.

A good customer whisperer has the good fortune of at least working within their species which allows them easier access to a deep well of empathy which increases trust between customer and service provider. The combination of empathy with effective communication becomes a superpower to the customer whisperer. Every interaction becomes a chance to wave your wand and leave a positive, lasting impression. In this way, you embody the affectionate customer whisperer you are.

Walking in Their Shoes

Empathy starts with our willingness to step into the shoes of the person we are interacting with. Imagine facing a challenging moment around someone who brushes you off, tells you not to worry about it, or worse, makes you feel like you are crazy? How might that feel?

Now take the same challenging moment and imagine experiencing this around someone who truly understands and shares your feelings. How does it feel? How might it feel to experience the opposite of this?

Empathy is not about understanding someone else because you've been there too; after all, every human has a unique perspective and lens covering their perceptions of experience. True empathy includes the ability to listen actively, and with full presence, to understand why the customer is thinking or behaving in a certain way. This is a way of attuning to the customer and gaining a clearer sense of their unique perspective. When you can understand this without judgment, the customer will feel heard and valued. Even if you disagree with them, the customer will still feel as if their emotions are valid.

Having empathy is what allows us to be truly kind and helpful to each other. Empathy in customer service looks like understanding and responding to the emotional needs of your customers. In customer service, walking in the customer's shoes means recognizing their emotions and experiences. When you approach customer service with empathy, you acknowledge the customer's feelings and work towards resolving their issues with care and compassion.

When it is appropriate in your role, you might think of yourself as a supportive friend who listens and offers help when needed. This approach not only resolves the immediate problem but also strengthens the overall relationship with the customer. By doing so, you can better address their concerns and provide solutions that resonate on a deeper level. This connection fosters trust and shows the customer that you genuinely care about their experience. Listening with true empathy goes a long way to helping your customers feel safe, and when they feel safe, trust can begin to grow.

Building empathy can take time, and if you are new to the concept or have not yet been exposed to empathy work, be patient and kind with yourself as you approach this. At the end of the day, empathy asks us to tap into our humanity, the condition we share with one another no matter our skin color, culture or other external differences. We are all human, which means we all have ideas, thoughts, feelings, needs and wants. Tapping into this is the beginning of connecting with empathy.

Here are several ways you can get started building this new muscle:

- **Avoid Assumptions – Seek True Understanding**: Don't assume you know what a customer is going through. Ask open-ended questions to understand their unique experience and address their actual concerns.

- **Stay Present and Practice Active Listening**: Focus fully on the customer during conversations. Use active listening by reflecting on what they say and providing non-verbal cues to show engagement.

- **Engage in Self-Care to Manage Your Own Biases**: Practice self-care to become aware of your triggers and biases. This helps you stay open-minded and ensures your reactions are fair and empathetic.

- **Avoid Over-Identification – Focus on Understanding**: Rather than commiserating or agreeing with a customer's frustration, focus on understanding their concerns. This helps maintain objectivity and address issues effectively.

- **Prioritize Understanding Before Problem-Solving**: Take time to fully understand the customer's perspective before jumping to solutions. This builds trust and ensures the solution truly meets their needs.

- **Recognize and Validate Emotions**: Acknowledge and validate the customer's emotions, whether positive or negative. This shows empathy and lays the foundation for constructive communication.

- **Practice Patience – Allow Space for the Customer's Story:** Give customers the time they need to express their concerns fully. Patience helps gather all the necessary details and makes the customer feel heard.

- **Reflect on Your Own Experiences**: Draw on your own experiences to better connect with customers. Use your reflections to guide empathetic responses while keeping the focus on their experience.

The Heartfelt Apology

An effective apology is more than just words; it's an expression of genuine regret and a commitment to make things right. Consider the difference between a perfunctory "I'm sorry" and a heartfelt apology that acknowledges the customer's feelings. The latter not only addresses the issue but also validates the customer's experience. A heartfelt apology, accompanied by actions to rectify the situation, can turn a negative experience into a positive one and rebuild trust.

While the scope of the book is about the relationship between customer and service provider, I will share the below story because it speaks to the transformational power a heartfelt apology could have. While you read it, allow your imagination to naturally make the necessary connections. Can you imagine how this kind of scenario and the way it led my employee to greater empathy might be doubly impactful in a customer-service provider interaction?

On a Saturday morning, tensions were running high in the hospitality industry where I worked part-time. Deadlines to have rooms ready by 11 a.m.

loomed, and the atmosphere was charged with the usual stresses of a competitive work environment. Among the team was Emily (name has been changed), a talented, experienced, but fiery employee known for her passion and dedication. However, on this day, Emily's passion morphed into something darker: anger.

It all started with a misunderstanding between Emily and her colleague Adella, who had always had a tense relationship. A minor disagreement over a room assignment escalated, and in a moment of frustration, Emily made a poor decision. She texted a derogatory message with harsh, hurtful words about Adella to Mannie, a new employee (but old friend), intending it as a private release of her anger. Unsure how to handle the situation, Mannie (name changed) shared the text with a few nearby colleagues, unintentionally fueling tensions in the hotel. In no time, the situation spread, sparking gossip and bad feelings. The once cohesive team began to fracture, with some defending Emily, calling it a lapse in judgment, while others sided with Adella, outraged by the unprovoked attack. The hotel, once a place of camaraderie and cooperation, became a battleground of whispers and cold stares. Productivity plummeted as the division grew, and the tension reached the ears of the housekeeping supervisor, Mrs. Helena (name changed). She knew she had to act quickly.

Upon learning of the issue, and after consulting with the HR manager, Mr. Thompson, Helena immediately met with Mannie to understand the situation and retrieve the text. She acknowledged her inexperience but emphasized the workplace policies she had violated, including the Respectful Workplace, Code of Conduct, and Confidentiality guidelines. Helena explained the consequences of her actions and stressed the importance of discretion and issued Mannie a verbal warning. Mannie, realizing her mistake, accepted the need for proper guidance and understood the impact her actions had on the team. She was provided with a copy of the hotel's code of conduct and was asked to sign off on it after reading it, leaving the meeting committed to improving her professionalism and workplace awareness.

Mr. Thompson immediately launched an investigation. Emily's actions, along with Mannie's decision to circulate the note, had created a toxic work environment and breached several workplace policies, such as inappropriate use of company time, Respectful Workplace, Code of Conduct, and confidentiality, among others. A formal disciplinary process was required. While Emily's support representative advocated for her, citing her strong work history and the stress she was under, Mr. Thompson had to balance this with the need to maintain a respectful and professional workplace.

After gathering all the facts and consulting with the hotel manager, Mr. Thompson made the difficult decision to issue Emily a written reprimand for her actions. The gravity of her mistake hit Emily hard. She realized that her impulsive, angry outburst had not only harmed Adella but also disrupted the entire hotel, resulting in a formal reprimand on her record.

As the reality of the situation set in, Emily felt a deep sense of remorse. She understood the gravity of her actions and the impact they had on her colleagues. Determined to make amends, she knew that a simple apology would not be enough. She needed to take full responsibility and make things right.

Emily decided to start with Adella. She knew it would be difficult, but she also knew it was necessary. She asked Adella to meet her in a quiet corner of the hotel, away from the prying eyes of their colleagues. When they sat down, Emily looked Adella in the eye and took a deep breath.

"Adella," she began, her voice trembling slightly, "I want to start by saying that I am truly, deeply sorry for what I did. There's no excuse for my actions and I understand how much they hurt you. I let my anger get the best of me and I wrote something that was cruel and untrue. I've reflected a lot on what happened, and I realize now how much damage I've caused—not just to you, but to the entire team. I don't expect you to forgive me right away, but I want you to know that I am committed to making this right, however I can."

Adella listened, her expression softening as she saw the genuine regret in Emily's eyes. In that moment, Emily could have left the apology at surface level, but something shifted inside her. She realized this was about more than just saying sorry—it was about truly understanding the person she had once disliked. Pausing for a moment, she looked at Adella, her voice quieter, more vulnerable. "Can you tell me more about what you're going through?" she asked. "I want to understand, not just apologize."

It was a powerful turning point—a moment of deep empathy, where Emily chose to set aside her past frustrations and open herself up to truly connect with someone she had struggled with.

Adella was surprised by the question, but she appreciated the opportunity to share her side. As they talked, Emily began to see a side of Adella she had never known. Adella spoke about the pressures she faced at home, the health issues of a close family member, and the cultural expectations that weighed heavily on her. She explained how these personal challenges sometimes spilled over into her work, making her seem aloof or unapproachable.

Emily felt a surge of empathy she hadn't expected. For the first time, she saw Adella not as a competitor but as a person with her own struggles and pain. She realized how her own actions had compounded Adella's stress and how unfair it had been to judge her without knowing her full story.

As their conversation continued, Emily shared some of her own experiences and challenges. The emotional connection they formed was powerful, transforming what could have been a routine apology into a meaningful engagement. Both women left that conversation with a deeper understanding and respect for each other.

This moment of vulnerability and honesty changed the dynamics between them. It turned what had been a transactional working relationship into a genuine friendship, built on trust and mutual respect. Emily's apology became more than just a step toward reconciliation. It became a bridge to a stronger, more compassionate workplace.

But Emily knew she had to do more. The rift her actions had caused in the hotel needed to be healed, and she wanted to take a public step toward making things right. At the end of the day, before going home, Mr. Thompson called for a quick team meeting. The atmosphere was tense as everyone filed in, unsure of what to expect.

The small room was a familiar setting for the team, typically reserved for team meetings and training sessions. But today, the room felt different, more charged, more significant. The table that usually fostered collaboration now seemed to emphasize the divide within the team. Emily stood at the head of the table, her heart pounding as she prepared to speak.

Taking a deep breath, Emily asked if she could address the small team. "I want to start by apologizing to all of you," she began, her voice steady despite the nervous energy coursing through her. "I made a terrible mistake, and I know I hurt not only Adella but all of you. My actions caused division, and I deeply regret the negative impact I've had on this hotel. I've already spoken with Adella privately, but I feel it's important to acknowledge this publicly."

She turned to Adella, who was sitting a few seats down. "Adella, I am so sorry for the pain I caused you. My words were hurtful and unjustified, and I take full responsibility for them. I hope you can forgive me."

The room was silent as everyone looked at Adella, waiting for her response. Adella stood up slowly, her eyes meeting Emily's. "Emily," she said, her voice clear and composed, "I appreciate your apology. It took a lot of courage to admit your mistake, and I respect that. I want you to know that I forgive you. Let's move forward from this and work together to rebuild the trust and unity in this hotel."

The tension in the room eased as Adella's words settled over to the team. There was a collective sigh of relief as the palpable rift between the two women began to mend in front of their eyes. Emily's public apology and Adella's public forgiveness were powerful symbols of reconciliation.

The meeting didn't end there. The hotel manager took the opportunity to address the entire team. "We all make mistakes," he said, looking around the room. "But it's how we respond to those mistakes that defines us. Emily's apology and Adella's forgiveness show us the strength of humility and the power of understanding."

He paused for a moment, then continued, "However, this situation also highlights the importance of fostering a healthy organizational culture. We cannot thrive if we allow frustration, resentment, or poor communication to take root. A strong, supportive culture is built on respect, empathy, and open dialogue. Each of us has a responsibility to contribute to that environment—whether by addressing issues before they escalate or supporting one another through challenges. Let this be a reminder that when we prioritize communication and empathy, we not only prevent conflicts but also create a workplace where everyone feels valued and heard."

He finished with a firm yet encouraging tone, "Moving forward, let's commit to working together in a way that strengthens our team and upholds the values of this organization."

As the meeting wrapped up, the mood in the boardroom had shifted. The division that had plagued the team was beginning to heal. Emily and Adella's relationship, once strained and adversarial, had transformed into something stronger, built on mutual respect and understanding. The team, too, felt the positive impact of this transformation, as they began to reconnect with one another in the days that followed.

Another benefit emerged from this situation. To prevent future breaches of confidentiality and to protect privacy, the hotel implemented a no use of cell phone during working hours. Employees could use their cell phones during breaks and lunches. This change not only increased hotel efficiency but also allowed the use of cell phones for personal matters outside of working hours. It was a simple yet effective solution that demonstrated the hotel's commitment to learning from its mistakes and creating a more secure and respectful work environment.

Emily's heartfelt apology, coupled with Adella's gracious public forgiveness, not only repaired the damage done but created a rippled effect that also transformed the entire team. By taking ownership of her actions and leading by example, Emily inspired others to reflect on their behavior. Mannie, deeply moved by the sincerity of Emily's apology, also stood up and apologized for her poor judgment in circulating the note. This collective act of accountability not only repaired the damage but also strengthened the bonds within the team, turning what had been a routine workplace conflict into a powerful journey of growth, reconciliation, and renewed respect.

The impact of this experience extended beyond the team and into their interactions with customers. The incident served as a profound reminder that colleagues are, in many ways, customers to each other, deserving of the same empathy, respect, and understanding. Emily, in particular, took this lesson to heart. She realized that her actions and words, whether with colleagues or customers, had the power to either harm or heal.

After the incident, Emily's approach to customer service changed significantly. She became more mindful of her words and actions, ensuring that she listened more intently and responded with empathy, even in challenging situations. She understood that an apology was not just a formality but a meaningful step toward rebuilding trust and strengthening relationships.

In another situation, in the same industry, at a much later date, a frustrated guest approached Emily when she went to clean her room with a complaint about how inconvenient the delayed service of the previous day was for her as her room was not ready as promised by 11 am. In the past, Emily might have responded defensively, but this time, she applied what she had learned. She listened carefully to the customer's concerns, acknowledged their frustration, and sincerely apologized for the inconvenience. "I'm truly sorry that we didn't meet your expectations," she said. "Your experience matters to us, and I want to make it right." The customer, initially agitated, softened in response to Emily's genuine apology and willingness to help. By the end of the conversation, not only was the issue resolved, but the customer also expressed appreciation for the way Emily handled the situation and gave Emily rave reviews on the hotel website.

This incident highlighted a key principle: that apologies, when given sincerely and with the intent to understand and rectify, can transform negative experiences into opportunities for building stronger, more loyal relationships. Emily's growth journey, from her conflict with Adella to her renewed approach with customers, reinforced the importance of empathy, accountability, and the power of a well-delivered apology in both internal and external customer service.

Building Trust and Loyalty with Every Customer

Trust and loyalty are the cornerstones of a successful customer relationship. Imagine a trusted friend who always has your back. That's the kind of relationship you want with your customers. Building this trust involves consistent, reliable service and always putting the customer's needs first. By demonstrating that you value and prioritize their satisfaction, you can foster loyalty that lasts.

In government, we did not have to work hard to engender loyalty because we were serving citizens, not typical customers as a business setting would produce. But that did not mean we didn't strive to create a feeling of trust and loyalty in everyone. In many ways, loyalty to us reflected loyalty to the government. While loyalty to government does not always correlate to engaged citizens of the kind a true functioning democracy needs, it does at least help the citizens feel better about coming to see us and being transparent with us when it comes to their needs and requests.

Loyalty in a business context is critical because it directly impacts a company's long-term success. Every brand aspires to cultivate customers who are not just satisfied but deeply committed, becoming true, devoted fans of the business. But how is this loyalty built? While there are many strategies to foster customer loyalty, at the core is the foundational relationship between the customer and the company. This relationship is nurtured through consistent, high-quality customer service.

Even as some large tech companies scale back on customer service, believing their size and market dominance will compensate, the reality is different for small businesses. Unlike big corporations, small businesses cannot afford to take customer loyalty for granted. For them, exceptional customer service isn't just a nice-to-have—it's a necessity. In a market where customers have numerous choices, the quality of service often becomes the deciding factor in whether a customer returns or seeks out a competitor. In this environment, outstanding customer service not only attracts new customers but also turns them into loyal advocates who continue to support and promote the business over time.

Ultimately, the investment in building strong customer relationships through excellent service pays dividends in the form of enduring customer loyalty—a loyalty that is far more essential to the survival and growth of a business than it might be for a government entity, where the customer base is often guaranteed.

The strongest ways to build trust and loyalty include developing empathy, as we discussed above, as well as two more key things: creating genuine connections, and communicating effectively.

Creating Genuine Connections

Building genuine, emotional connections with customers goes beyond transactional interactions. It's about creating moments of genuine understanding and support. Think of the bond between old friends who can communicate without words; this is a genuine connection built on trust, respect and shared experiences. In customer service, these connections are built through attentive listening, sincere responses, and recognizing the customer's individual and unique perspective and needs. Emotional connections transform routine transactions into meaningful engagements that leave a lasting impact.

Creating genuine connections with customers involves authenticity and openness. It's like having a meaningful conversation with a friend where both parties feel understood and valued. In customer service, this means being real and relatable. Share your name, show empathy, and be approachable. Genuine connections are built on honesty and mutual respect, which can significantly enhance customer satisfaction and loyalty.

Horse whisperers build emotional connections like these with their horses when they practice mirroring or matching the horse's energy. It is through building a genuine connection that trust can continue growing between horse and trainer.

Building an emotional connection between a horse and trainer is typically both safe and beneficial, as it occurs within the boundaries of an inter-species relationship. However, when two humans form emotional connections, the situation becomes more complex and requires careful attention to boundaries and appropriate behavior. Without a clear understanding of these elements, emotional connections can easily be misinterpreted, leading to unintended consequences.

For example, consider a young woman behind the counter who is naturally charming and friendly to everyone she meets. While her warmth is a valuable trait, it could be misinterpreted by a male customer who has difficulty discerning social cues, such as someone on the autism spectrum. He might mistake her friendliness for flirtation or develop an inappropriate attachment. In such cases, even well-intentioned emotional connections could lead to discomfort or harm for both individuals involved. This highlights the delicate balance required when building emotional connections in customer service. The type of interaction, setting, and nature of the service all play significant roles in determining whether such connections should be formed. In some business environments, forming emotional connections may be inappropriate or even counterproductive. However, in settings like the developmental services home where I worked as a residential counsellor, empathy and understanding are crucial. In these environments, emotional connections can greatly benefit both the service provider and the customer.

Ultimately, the key is to understand when and how to build emotional connections, ensuring they serve to enhance the customer experience without crossing any lines or leading to misunderstandings. This delicate work requires constant attention to context, the individual needs of customers, and the professional boundaries that safeguard both parties.

Effective Communication

In Chapter 2, we discussed the value of effective communication and specific communication techniques like active listening. Effective communication is crucial in setting the foundation for a positive customer relationship, as it sets the tone and creates a container for the interaction to take place within. When the customer understands the rules and boundaries from the start of the interaction, they automatically feel safer, and from that safety, trust can begin to emerge.

Keeping the customer informed is a way of managing their expectations and keeping them realistic. Here are some more ways to communicate effectively in the moment of interaction:

- Ask questions to ensure they understand your role and responsibilities.

- Repeat their words back to them to confirm the message is not mixed.

- Provide customers with a copy of their obligations, or post customer expectations on your store window or website.

- Use corresponding body language and eye contact that is congruent with your spoken words.

- Make sure to maintain eye contact and use open, welcoming gestures.

- If you are explaining a complicated process, nod your head and maintain a steady gaze. This conveys confidence and clarity.

For bonuses go to www.thecustomerwhispererbook.com

Top Three Takeaways

Whenever you wave your wand as a customer whisperer, you are harnessing the magic within to transform complaints into heartfelt compliments. Add empathy and effective communication to this and you truly have superpowers.

Empathy and effective communication are essential for excellence in customer service, allowing you to transform complaints into compliments.

Build trust and meaningful connections by being genuine, relatable, and offering heartfelt apologies when needed.

Use clear communication, ask questions to confirm understanding, and set realistic expectations to foster loyalty and prioritize the customer's needs.

Chapter 7
Turning Anger Into Appreciation

"To hear complaints with patience, even when complaints are vain, is one of the duties of friendship."
– Samuel Johnson

7

thought it was an ordinary day in my self-employed role as personal support worker when I went into Mitchel's home to support him. Although Mitchel (name changed) was usually subdued when we got together, today he was an extremely irate customer. On this day, Mitchel, who had an acquired brain injury while still in his prime, stormed around his home, his anger fueled with deep-seated frustration about his situation. His face was flushed with anger, his voice loud enough to draw the attention of neighbors. His frustration was palpable, and the tension in the room grew as he continued to voice his grievances.

Mitchel, a Behavioral Psychology graduate, faced significant challenges due to severe social anxiety and occasional panic attacks, which prevented him from securing or maintaining employment in his chosen field. Despite his education and skills, his condition made it difficult to engage confidently in professional settings, especially in situations requiring public speaking or presenting ideas. His anxiety often led to avoidance of social interactions, including job interviews and networking, which are crucial for building a career in Behavioral Psychology. This left him feeling frustrated and resentful, particularly as the burden of student loans weighed heavily on him.

Whenever I met with Mitchel, he often expressed frustration, sometimes comparing himself to me, believing he was more qualified. His dissatisfaction was clear, but I recognized that his anger masked a deeper struggle. With a calm demeanor, I approached him, understanding that defusing the situation was just the beginning. As a true "customer whisperer," I could see that Mitchel's frustrations were rooted in his internal battle with anxiety and unmet expectations.

We usually met at a café, and I would guide him to a quieter, more private spot where we could talk openly. During these conversations, I listened carefully, not only to his words but to the pain and anxiety that lay beneath them. Maintaining eye contact and offering a safe space, I said, "Mitchel, I can see you're upset, and I want to understand what's really going on. Let's talk about it so we can find a solution together."

As Mitchel began to share his frustrations, I engaged fully, acknowledging his feelings. I told him, "I understand why you're upset, and I'm here to work through this with you." My empathy allowed him to feel truly heard, perhaps for the first time in a long while. I could see that Mitchel needed more than just a friend to talk to; he needed professional support to help him manage his anxiety and career challenges.

I referred him to a vocational rehabilitation specialist I knew, someone who occasionally worked pro bono and could offer the right guidance. This was a pivotal moment—where my ability to look beyond the immediate frustration and provide meaningful support set Mitchel on a path toward healing and growth.

With time, and under the specialist's care, Mitchel began receiving Cognitive Behavioral Therapy and practicing gratitude—a key element that contributed to his transformation. I continued meeting with him regularly, encouraging him through the process. Gradually, Mitchel's anxiety diminished, his confidence grew, and the once-insurmountable barriers in his life began to fade away.

Defusing Tense Situations

When it comes to anger, humans and animals differ greatly. After all, have you ever really seen an angry animal? It's likelier you may have seen a hungry animal, baring fangs as it bore down on its prey; this is not necessarily anger at all.

In contrast, humans experience anger whenever they feel unheard, unsafe, uncomfortable, or have other basic needs unmet. Anger is often an unconscious reaction; there are hordes of humans out there reacting angrily at any given moment, often with a complete lack of awareness as to why they are truly angry. It might be that all they need is some food or hydration, yet they take their anger out on whomever is nearby. When people experience chronic anger and angry outbursts, it's worth checking in to see how their self-care has been that day. Often a quick break to go outside, a drink of water, a snack is all it takes to bring someone back to a non-angry state.

Customers presenting with anger are likely feeling a sense of stress, fear, or anxiety beneath the anger. When it comes to horses, they too feel stress and anxiety, which is part of what a horse whisperer seeks to allay. While horses do not present as "angry" like a human might, they do have their own challenging behaviors when they first begin training with a horse whisperer.

Horse whisperers thus utilize their skills, many of which we've touched on throughout the book. They use mirroring, to gain the horse's trust. They communicate non-verbally and verbally in effective ways, softly and gently, to alleviate stress and anxiety. Many horse whispering techniques are purposely designed to manage aggression in the animal, often caused by fear. Horse whisperers must learn to face their own fears of aggression in animals so they can be calm in front of the horse and keep both the horse and them safe. This deepens trust and increases safety for both horse and trainer.

When dealing with an angry customer, the first step is to try to defuse or de-escalate the situation. Picture a full-to-the-brim pot of water on a stove. If you do not lower the heat, the water will overflow once it begins boiling.

Bring your calm and composed demeanor to a customer who is angry is the same as turning that stove burner down. It will at least introduce a calmness to the interaction and can help reduce the customer's anger, as I did, listening actively, acknowledging the customer's feelings, and responding with empathy. Using non-violent communication tactics, notably "I" statements, is also helpful in calming a situation. To do this, instead of starting any sentences with "you," the customer whisperer seeks to start with "I." For example, "I hear you," and "I understand" go a long way when trying to get to a constructive conversation.

In the human services field, most angry customers have a very real need attached to their anger. By this I mean, these are people depending on the support of others to live fulfilled lives. If they feel angry, there is often an existential fear connected to this; those supports are their lifeline.

Contrast this to the person who is just trying to buy an article of clothing in a retail environment. Chances are good in the latter situation that the person is angry because they're tired or busy or hungry or thirsty.

Whether working in a retail business, a large corporation, or a government services agency, angry customers will arise from time to time. Understanding how anger works in humans and seeking to show up with empathy, using your effective communication superpowers, is how you become a customer whisperer.

The Transformation

One afternoon, several months after that intense day mentioned above, I met with Mitchel again at the usual restaurant and found that he was a completely different person. Gone was the anger that once filled his eyes. Instead, he walked calmly and purposefully.

I immediately noticed the change in Mitchel. With a warm smile, I approached him, eager to learn what had sparked such a profound transformation. Mitchel explained that after our previous encounter, he had taken my kind yet impactful words to heart and followed up on my recommendation to see the vocational rehabilitation specialist, who recognizing that Mitchel could benefit from CBT, referred him to a qualified mental health professional. The transformation occurred when Mitchel, with the help of a dedicated therapist, began a comprehensive treatment plan that included cognitive-behavioral therapy (CBT), gradual exposure to the situations that triggered his anxiety and a daily practice of gratitude. Over time, he learned to manage his symptoms more effectively, reducing their impact on his daily life. As his confidence grew and his anxiety diminished, the barriers that once hindered his career began to disappear and he became even more grateful for his overall improved well-being.

Eventually, Mitchel was able to apply his skills and knowledge in a professional setting, secure employment in his chosen field, and thrive in a role that once seemed out of reach. The contrast between his earlier struggles and his later success underscores the profound impact that managing his disability had on his professional life, making his journey all the more compelling and inspiring.

This simple shift had a ripple effect on every aspect of his life. His mindset became more positive, and his attitude shifted from frustration to optimism. As he practiced gratitude, he noticed that his words became more encouraging, his actions more considerate, and his feelings more balanced. As a result, people around him started treating him differently, friends and family began to respect him more, his relationships grew stronger, and even strangers responded to him with kindness. Mitchel shared how opportunities that once seemed out of reach began to appear, from unexpected job offers to new friendships. His whole life experience transformed in an instant, as he embraced the continuous practice of gratitude, leading to a life filled with positivity and growth.

"I realized that being angry wasn't helping me," Mitchel said. "But when I started focusing on what I was grateful for, everything changed. I found peace, and that peace led me to a new path."

Mitchel went on to share how this newfound peace had led him to secure a job at a social service agency. He was now in a position where he could help others, just as Mandy had helped him. "I don't need your supports anymore. Thank you for all you have done for me," he said with a smile. "I'm giving back, and it feels incredible."

The Art of Gratitude

Weeks later, Mitchel reached out to me, not as a client but as a colleague eager to share the journey and techniques that had transformed his life. I was so moved by his story that I immediately contacted Mandy, the vocational rehabilitation specialist to share the good news. The specialist was thrilled and invited Mitchel to present his story to the team.

Mitchel's presentation was nothing short of dynamic, blending personal testimony, practical advice, and inspirational storytelling. From the moment he began, the audience was captivated by his energy and authenticity. He recounted his own experiences, starting with a day when he had a stormy outburst of anger and frustration during an encounter with me. Mitchel spoke openly about his emotions and feelings of helplessness despite his qualifications in Behavioral Psychology. His raw honesty resonated deeply with the audience, many of whom had likely encountered similar situations in their work.

Mitchel's transformation was not just a personal journey but a testament to the power of gratitude and the impact of a single compassionate act. When he addressed my colleagues, it was clear that his success was deeply connected to the guidance and insight I had provided as a "customer whisperer." I had seen beyond his anger to the deeper issues he was grappling with.

During his talk, Mitchel emphasized the pivotal role I played in his transformation. He shared how my calm and empathetic approach during our initial encounter helped him get the support he truly needed. He explained that I recognized his frustration was rooted in deeper struggles with anxiety and self-worth. My referral to a vocational rehabilitation specialist sparked his path to recovery and success.

Mitchel credited much of his success to the wisdom I shared and to his practice of gratitude, which his therapist had introduced, and I had encouraged. This simple practice became central to his healing, helping him shift his focus from what was lacking in his life to what he had. His story demonstrated the broader impact of "customer whispering"—turning negative experiences into positive, life-changing moments.

As Mitchel's presentations gained popularity, he stressed that this approach was not just about resolving immediate concerns—it was about transforming lives. He encouraged his audience to see their interactions as opportunities for lasting change, using gratitude and understanding to help others find peace and fulfillment, even in difficult circumstances.

Mitchel shared that my influence had not only changed his life but was now touching the lives of many others. What began as a personal journey had grown into a movement, embodying the essence of "customer whispering" by turning complaints into compliments and creating positive change.

In his presentations, Mitchel made it clear that I had gone beyond the call of duty. All he initially sought was someone to talk to, a companion to share a coffee with occasionally. He appreciated that I didn't just see an angry individual—I saw a person in pain, struggling beneath the surface with challenges far greater than what was apparent. My actions were a true example of what it means to be a "customer whisperer." I didn't just resolve his immediate concerns; I took the time to understand the root of his frustration and guided him toward the support that would ultimately transform his life.

By recognizing that Mitchel needed more than a quick solution, I demonstrated the profound impact of going beyond what is expected. I listened not just to his words but to his unspoken needs, offering the kind of support that extended far beyond my formal responsibilities. This level of care and dedication was what Mitchel credited for his transformation.

My willingness to go the extra mile made all the difference, showing that sometimes, the most powerful change comes not from doing what is required, but from doing what is right. My actions embodied the core message of the book—the power of empathy, understanding, and a touch of gratitude to turn even the most challenging situations into opportunities for growth and transformation.

Spiritual and Other Benefits of Gratitude

Although I wasn't able to assist Mitchel in the heat of the moment when he was an angry customer, my referral to the vocational specialist ultimately helped him find the support he needed.

It was then up to Mitchel to apply that practice and allow it to transform him. By choosing to do so, he underwent a mindset shift, moving from being an angry customer to eventually becoming a "customer whisperer" himself over time.

This is just one example of how expressing gratitude can transform a negative interaction into a positive one. Think of gratitude as an ointment that soothes wounds. Thank the customer for bringing the issue to your attention and for their patience as you work towards a solution. Gratitude shows that you value their feedback and are committed to improving their experience. This approach not only addresses the immediate concern but also leaves a lasting positive impression.

Gratitude goes beyond just being polite; it has profound spiritual and personal benefits. Spiritually, gratitude fosters a sense of connectedness and purpose. It can make you feel more aligned with your values and more attuned to the positive aspects of life. This mindset can lead to a deeper sense of fulfillment and inner peace, as we saw happened to Mitchel.

In my personal experience, practicing gratitude has significantly improved my overall well-being. It has helped reduce stress, enhanced my mood, and increased my resilience. By focusing on the positive aspects of my interactions and expressing gratitude, I've noticed a positive shift not only in my mental health but also in the environment around me. Gratitude has acted as a buffer against negative emotions and helped me build stronger, more supportive relationships.

In the workplace, a culture of gratitude can lead to higher levels of employee satisfaction and engagement. When employees feel appreciated, they are more likely to be motivated and committed to their work. This positive energy can enhance teamwork and collaboration, leading to better outcomes for the organization.

Remarkable Heights

This chapter illustrates the power of gratitude, the importance of maintaining a calm demeanor in tense situations, and how one person's transformation can lead to greater changes within a community.

Fast forward two decades later, Mitchel's journey of transformation and growth has led him to remarkable heights. He has gone into business for himself as a behavioral psychologist, a role that perfectly aligns with his passion and expertise. His business is flourishing, offering services that focus on helping others overcome challenges through the power of gratitude, positive thinking, and effective communication.

For bonuses go to ...

Mitchel's reputation has grown far beyond the walls of his former workplace. He has become a renowned speaker, sought after by organizations and conferences around the world to share his inspiring story and insights. His dynamic presentations, filled with personal anecdotes and practical advice, continue to captivate audiences and leave a lasting impact. Mitchel's success is a testament to the power of resilience, gratitude, and the belief that with the right mindset, any challenge can be turned into an opportunity for growth.

Mitchel's story perfectly encapsulates the themes of both this chapter and the entire book. His journey from anger and frustration to appreciation and success demonstrates the transformative power of empathy, gratitude, and positive communication. By embracing these principles, Mitchel not only turned his own life around but also became a beacon of hope for others. His story is a shining example of what it means to be a customer whisperer, someone who can take the most challenging situations, whether it's a complaint, a conflict, or a personal struggle, and, with a wave of a compassionate and understanding wand, turn them into opportunities for connection, growth, lasting positive change and compliments.

Top Three Takeaways

As a compassionate and special customer whisperer, wave your wand to turn complaints into compliments, embodying the true essence of customer service excellence that this book champions.

Defuse Tense Situations with Empathy and Calm: Approach tense interactions with empathy and composure to de-escalate anger and create a constructive dialogue.

Harness Gratitude to Create Memorable Moments: Express gratitude to transform dissatisfaction into appreciation, leaving a lasting positive impact and fostering customer loyalty.

Personalize Service and Foster a Culture of Gratitude: Tailor service to each customer's unique needs, ensuring they feel valued and respected. Gratitude strengthens both customer relationships and workplace culture.

Chapter 8
Embracing Diversity, Inclusion, Equity, and Accessibility

"Be the change you wish to see in the world."
– Mahatma Gandhi, Leader of Indian Independence Movement

8

Horse whispering is connected to a form of training known as natural horsemanship. The approach is very different to the old-fashioned way of training horses by breaking them using brute force. Instead, horse whisperers use psychology to motivate the horse they are training. Unlike humans, horses have motivations too, and a good horse whisperer will deduce this and leverage it.

In the horse world, there is no such thing as diversity, inclusion, equity and accessibility, yet each of these still plays a role in the ring. The horse and trainer themselves are diverse, two species communicating with one another. The horse must allow the trainer into the ring in the first place, an inclusion on the part of the animal. The horse and trainer are on the same level as they work together, which nods to equity. And the horse and trainer are also always in a space that is conducive to quality work, the horse is in an accessible, comfortable environment in which it feels safe.

Horse whisperers working with a natural horsemanship style seek to maintain a calm demeanor, to respect and understand the animal and the animal's unique "horse-onality" (so to speak). This is why I have drawn on this analogy throughout the book; a good customer whisperer is really going to capitalize on the skills a horse whisperer demonstrates.

Imagine the new horse whisperer working with a huge, black stallion. The horse is tall, wild, and the whisperer a tiny woman. Do you believe that tiny woman can tame that stallion using brute force only? Not a chance. But she can enter the space softly and calmly, defer to the horse by understanding the psychology and herd mentality of horses, and mirror the horse's behavior to create safety and gain respect. Natural horsemanship is about using subtle, often non-verbal, signals to communicate between horse and human. Body language often sends the loudest messages to horses.

Whether you are a petite woman training a might stallion, or a customer service provider facing an enraged customer, the similarities are obvious. In the face of a big beast who might be an angry person, or a person with a different cultural background, or even a person who is in a wheelchair, how can you ensure you show up with calmness, respect and a genuine heart of service, knowing you are there to help them to the best of your ability? This chapter will show you the pathway to excellence in diversity, equity and inclusion (DEI) as well as accessibility.

Creating an Accessible, Welcoming, and Comfortable Environment

Creating a positive customer experience starts with setting the right environment. Among the first things a horse whisperer does is ensure the physical space is safe, and their demeanor is welcoming and calm. This is precisely what a good customer whisperer does, too. A clean, organized, and comfortable environment can put customers at ease. Equally important is providing emotional comfort by showing warmth, patience, and understanding. This dual approach helps to create a positive and supportive atmosphere for customers, making them feel valued and respected from the moment they interact with you.

For all the agencies in the human services field, including government agencies that I worked for, we made every effort to create a positive, accessible and welcoming environment in which to serve our customers.

Before diversity and inclusion became widely recognized concepts, in the early 2000s, a young man named Kevin (name changed), who was visually impaired, approached me after Sunday church service, during our social gathering, seeking help with completing an application for a guide dog. I quickly realized that the standard printed forms wouldn't be accessible for him. Without hesitation, I offered to read the forms aloud and assist him in filling them out. Additionally, I ensured that Kevin could access audio resources on his portable CD player, helping him find relevant materials that detailed the services available to him. By adapting my approach to meet Kevin's unique needs, I demonstrated a commitment to inclusivity, even before it was a formal focus. Kevin was so appreciative of the personalized support that he wrote me a letter of commendation, praising how I accommodated his diverse needs. When I asked why he had chosen me for help, he said he recognized my voice from when I offered him the host during holy communion, in my volunteer role of Eucharist Minister.

Celebrating This Success: Kevin discovered where I worked and sent a copy of his letter to my manager. My dedication to accessibility was recognized during a staff meeting, where my efforts were highlighted as a model of inclusive service, even when off duty. Following this, the organization launched an "Accessibility Champion" program and invited me to join the committee. The program encouraged staff to share innovative ideas for improving accessibility for all customers. Kevin's story was also featured in the local office newsletter, showcasing our commitment to inclusivity and accessibility.

The many organizations I worked for all took pride in creating a space where every customer feels welcomed, valued, and at ease. That is what I liked about working in the human services field. Understanding that a positive customer experience begins with the environment, these organizations put considerable thought into both the physical layout of their service centers and the demeanor with which they greet each customer.

The story begins with the renovation of my personal music room at home, where I taught piano lessons. My first student was a young person in a wheelchair, which inspired me to make the space more accessible and inviting for him and all my students. Upon entering, customers are greeted by a bright, clean, and well-organized reception area. The walls display artwork by local artists, celebrating the diversity of our community. Comfortable seating is thoughtfully arranged, with chairs designed to accommodate individuals of all sizes and abilities. The space is well-lit, and clear, multilingual signs ensure a welcoming environment for everyone.

Since I had a student who used a wheelchair, I paid special attention to accessibility. When I bought my home in the early 1980s, I specifically sought out a house with a ramp and wide doorways to make entry easy for those with mobility challenges. In one corner of the waiting area, I created a quiet space for students to work on their music theory assignments while waiting for their practical session. This area features softer lighting, calming colors, and comfortable seating, providing a peaceful and relaxing retreat.

The welcoming environment extended to the small details as well. Fresh flowers were placed on the table each week, and a water cooler with disposable cups was available for customers. These small touches contribute to an atmosphere of care and consideration, making customers feel that their comfort is a priority.

Equity and accessibility are crucial to delivering high-quality service to all customers. Human services organizations frequently provide accommodations and adjustments to meet specific needs, such as offering documents in Braille for visually impaired individuals or sign language interpreters for deaf customers. Employees receive training on accessibility to stay informed about the resources available to support customers with special needs. Making use of these accessible resources is key to providing an inclusive and respectful service, ensuring that every customer enjoys an equitable experience. By creating an accessible and welcoming environment, organizations establish a strong foundation for diversity and inclusion, both of which are essential elements of exceptional customer service.

Celebrating Diversity in Customer Service

Celebrating diversity involves recognizing and valuing the different perspectives and experiences that each customer brings. Imagine a tapestry woven from many different threads; each thread adds to the richness of the design. In customer service, this means being open to different viewpoints and adapting your approach to meet diverse needs. By celebrating diversity, you not only enrich the customer experience but also build a more inclusive and supportive service environment.

To deepen your approach to diversity and inclusion, it helps to get a handle on the basics of human behavior and psychology. Each human is full of biases and assumptions, with racist imprints from past cultural influences still lingering in the minds of many. Let's look at how understanding human behavior can fuel a stronger commitment to diversity and inclusion in customer service.

Understanding Human Behavior

An understanding of human behavior is the cornerstone of excellent customer service. People behave differently based on their cultural backgrounds, beliefs, religion, gender, physical health, emotional well-being, mental health, and other factors. These differences stem from varied experiences and perspectives. Imagine trying to solve a puzzle without knowing the picture you are trying to create. By understanding what drives people, their motivations, and their emotions, you can better predict and respond to their needs. This knowledge helps you tailor your approach, so it is customized for everyone, making your service more effective and personalized. Recognizing and respecting these differences fosters a more compassionate and inclusive environment where everyone feels valued. When differences are embraced, it enriches the environment, leading to a more vibrant, dynamic, and innovative community.

For bonuses go to ...

As I look back on my childhood, I vividly recall seeing other children who were often alone, with no friends to share their time with, isolated on the playground or sitting by themselves in the cafeteria. At the time, I didn't fully understand why they were so often on the fringes of social circles, seemingly invisible to the rest of us. They were the ones who didn't get invited to birthday parties, who were picked last for teams, and who spent recess wandering alone.

Now, with the wisdom that comes from years of life experience, I see these same individuals in adulthood, and the picture is much clearer, though far more heartbreaking. Many of those children who were once isolated have grown into adults who struggle with deep-seated issues. Some have turned to addictions—alcohol, drugs, smoking, or even overeating—to cope with the pain of exclusion and the lingering feelings of inadequacy that began in childhood. These vices have become their escape from the harsh reality of a world where they've always felt like outsiders.

It's clear that the isolation they experienced as children left scars that never fully healed. Instead of blossoming into the best versions of themselves, these individuals often find themselves trapped in a cycle of self-destructive behaviors, unable to break free from the patterns established in their formative years. They've missed out on reaching their full potential, not because they lacked the ability, but because the emotional wounds from their childhood were never properly addressed.

As I reflect on this, it underscores the profound impact that childhood experiences of exclusion can have on an individual's entire life. It's a stark reminder of the importance of creating inclusive environments where every child—and every adult—feels valued and supported, so that they can grow into their fullest, most authentic selves.

In the context of diversity and inclusion, when a customer feels excluded or marginalized due to their background, culture, or identity, a range of effects and impacts can be presented. For many, the situation reactivates a childhood trauma, leaving them reacting from a place of feeling trapped in a vicious cycle of exclusion and marginalization. This ongoing experience of being undervalued and overlooked can prevent them from moving forward and fully participating in society if it is not seen and validated by a supportive person or even therapist if required. The harm isn't just immediate—it's a painful reminder of past wounds that have never fully healed.

Addressing the root causes of these feelings—whether in a playground, in a social service setting, or within an organization—requires understanding, empathy, and proactive inclusion. By making everyone feel welcome and valued, and by addressing these deep-seated issues with care and support, we can help individuals break free from this cycle and create a more inclusive environment where everyone can reach their full potential.

But what stops a person from being able to extend this kind of grace and care to another? Often, it is the unconscious biases we carry around, which were often just things influencing us, like the culture we were raised within, that we are still reacting to without questioning. How can we learn to address these biases so we can show up with more openness?

Addressing Bias

Learning about our biases and taking action to eliminate them is essential in promoting a culture of fairness and respect. It is important to recognize that everyone has biases that are commonly born of cultural, societal or familial influences around us growing up. Without ever examining these with conscious awareness, most people unconsciously react to these biases in their interactions and decisions. By educating ourselves and others, we can become more aware of our own biases and work to mitigate their impact.

One way of educating others is by respectfully calling out bias when we see it, helping to create an environment where everyone feels valued and respected. This proactive approach not only improves individual interactions but also fosters a more inclusive and equitable service culture. The dark side to this approach, however, is when a person is unaware of their own biases. Then, this calling out is projection, and is often unhelpful for all parties involved. Calling out other people on their biases can also be extremely triggering to the other, especially when not done sensitively or when done with a self-righteous, holier-than-thou approach. This dance is a delicate one, and the ideal starting point is by investigating one's own biases first to ensure awareness and diminish the risk of projection.

Recognizing and Calling Out Bias

In the human services field, promoting a culture of fairness and respect is not just a goal, it's a commitment. Understanding that biases, whether conscious or unconscious, can subtly influence our interactions and decisions, human services agencies make it a priority to address these biases head-on. The journey toward a more inclusive and equitable service culture begins with education and is reinforced through action.

The story begins with a casual conversation that a student reported to me in 1989 while I was working as an occasional supply teacher. She had overheard a group of students I was supervising discussing a recent interaction with another classmate. During the conversation, Sariah (name changed), a high school student, noticed that her peer, Andray (name changed), had unintentionally made a biased remark about another student's background, assuming the challenges that student faced were due to their ethnicity. Recognizing that the comment was inappropriate, though not fully understanding the bias, Sariah felt a responsibility to address it but knew it was important to do so respectfully and constructively.

After recess, Sariah approached Andray privately. She gently explained how the remark could be perceived as racist and how such assumptions could damage relationships with classmates and undermine the school's sense of integrity. Andray, though initially surprised, listened attentively and ultimately appreciated Sariah's thoughtful approach. He hadn't realized the impact of his words and thanked her for bringing it to his attention. This conversation not only helped Andray become more aware of his own biases but also strengthened the trust and openness between him and his peers.

When I learned of this upon returning to the classroom, I seized the opportunity to educate the students about creating a respectful environment centered around diversity, inclusion, and recognizing bias. We had a brief but meaningful discussion about unconscious biases, their effects, and strategies to counteract them. I also took the opportunity to inform the high school principal, hoping it would spark a broader conversation with students.

During the five-minute discussion, the students admitted they had been unaware of the impact of their actions and began to uncover some of their own unconscious biases. These conversations were eye-opening, as they began to see how subtle biases could infiltrate their daily interactions. At the end of the school day, I reported my findings to the principal, who expressed interest in addressing the issue in a constructive way, much like Sariah did with Andray. I encouraged the principal to implement role-playing scenarios to help students practice how to address bias when they encounter it, ensuring they feel confident and equipped to handle such situations in the future.

Calling Out Bias at a Team Meeting

During a team meeting, Mr. Roberto (name changed) emphasized the importance of inclusion and respect. This is how he handled both a subtle and overt act of exclusion:

- **Subtle Act of Exclusion:** When Monique (name changed), an administrative secretary, suggested an idea, Chris (name changed) subtly dismissed it by suggesting the task was too technical for some people.

After noticing this, Mr. Roberto privately told Chris, "I noticed that Monique had a valid point earlier, but it seemed like the conversation moved past it. Let's make sure we give her a chance to explain the customer's perspective more clearly."

- **Overt Act of Exclusion:** Later, when Chris interrupted Monique again, dismissing her perspective, Mr. Roberto directly addressed the exclusion, saying, "Chris, I think it's important we hear Monique out. The customer perspective is crucial to the success of this rollout, and we need every angle to be fully considered. Let's give her the floor to finish her thoughts." This reinforced the message that exclusionary actions wouldn't be tolerated and that every contribution mattered.

By doing this, Mr. Roberto addressed the behavior head-on, ensuring that Monique's contributions were respected and that everyone in the room recognized that exclusionary actions wouldn't be tolerated. Mr. Roberto called out the bias directly, and also refocused the conversation on the importance of collaboration and respect.

Continuous Learning and Commitment to Improvement

The bias awareness training is just the beginning. The human services agency is committed to ongoing learning and improvement, understanding that addressing bias is not a one-time effort but a continuous journey. The leadership team implements regular check-ins and refresher courses on bias, ensuring that the lessons learned are reinforced over time. Additionally, the office creates a safe space for open dialogue, where staff can share their experiences and discuss how to handle challenging situations involving bias.

To further embed the principles of fairness and respect into the office culture, a Bias Review Committee is established. This committee, composed of staff from various levels and backgrounds, meets regularly to review practices, policies, and customer interactions through the lens of bias. They provide recommendations for improvements and serve as a resource for colleagues who may need support in addressing bias-related issues.

The Impact on Customer Service

As a result of these efforts, the human services agency is beginning to see a noticeable change in how customers are treated. Staff members approach their work with greater awareness and sensitivity, leading to more equitable and respectful interactions. Customers from diverse backgrounds report feeling more understood and valued, as their unique needs and perspectives are better recognized and addressed.

The office also starts receiving positive feedback from the community. Local organizations that serve marginalized groups commend the agency for its proactive stance on addressing bias and fostering an inclusive environment. This feedback reinforces the team's commitment to continuous improvement and motivates them to keep pushing toward even higher standards of fairness and respect.

This narrative demonstrates how recognizing, calling out, and addressing bias through education and continuous learning creates a more inclusive and equitable service culture at the agency. It highlights the importance of proactive measures and the positive impact they have on both staff and customers.

Inclusive Excellence

Inclusive excellence means providing outstanding service to every customer, regardless of their cultural background and ethnicity. Picture a garden with a variety of flowers; each one adds beauty to the whole. In customer service, this means acknowledging and respecting diversity and ensuring that every customer feels welcome and valued. Inclusive practices enhance the overall customer experience and demonstrate a commitment to equity and respect. With every wave of your all-inclusive wand, you sprinkle extraordinary confetti of respect, positivity, and appreciation, like the supportive customer whisperer you are.

At a local human services agency, our monthly celebrations of cultural and religious diversity have become more than just festive events; they have become a cornerstone of inclusive excellence. Each staff member enthusiastically prepares for these celebrations, excited to not only share their heritage but be part of fostering a deeper understanding and respect for the diverse backgrounds of their colleagues. This will then ripple out into a respect and appreciation for all the cultural diaspora their customers represent.

For instance, when Anna-Maria (name change) leads the celebration for Hispanic Heritage Month, the team's exposure to her Mexican culture extends beyond the office walls. The insights shared during the event help staff members better understand and connect with their Hispanic customers. By learning about Anna-Maria's traditions, language nuances, and the cultural significance of certain practices, her colleagues develop a deeper empathy and a more tailored approach to serving Hispanic customers. This cultural competence translates into more empathetic and effective service, ensuring that customers feel understood and respected.

Similarly, Bendigo's (name change) celebration of Black History Month not only educates his colleagues about the significant contributions of Black Canadians but also deepens their commitment to addressing the systemic barriers that customers from Black communities may face. The knowledge gained from the local historian's talk and Bendigo's personal stories inspires the staff to be more vigilant in identifying and dismantling biases within their service processes. This heightened awareness leads to more equitable treatment of all customers, regardless of their background, reinforcing the office's dedication to inclusive excellence.

During the Diwali celebration, Priya's (name change) efforts to share her culture with her colleagues have a lasting impact. The spiritual and cultural understanding gained from the prayer ceremony and the stories behind the traditions encourage staff to approach their work with greater sensitivity to the religious and cultural practices of their customers. This awareness is particularly important when working with customers who observe religious rituals or need accommodation during certain times of the year. By understanding Priya's experience, the staff become more adept at anticipating and respecting the diverse religious needs of their customers, which enhances the overall quality of service.

These celebrations go beyond food, decorations, and learning and translate directly into how the staff serve their diverse customers. By understanding the diverse backgrounds and experiences of their colleagues, staff members develop the skills and cultural sensitivity necessary to appreciate and serve their customers better. They recognize that each customer, like their colleagues, brings a unique set of cultural, religious, and life experiences to the table. This understanding helps staff to approach each customer interaction with greater empathy, patience, and respect, creating a more inclusive and supportive service environment.

Beyond the individual celebrations, the practice of inviting experts from the community to lead discussions and share insights has become a model for continuous learning and improvement. These interactions provide staff with the knowledge and tools they need to serve customers from diverse backgrounds with excellence. The office has also established ongoing partnerships with these community leaders, ensuring that their expertise is integrated into training programs and service delivery strategies:

- **Cultural Liaison Programs** connect the office with cultural leaders who bridge the gap between service providers and communities, ensuring culturally appropriate service delivery and tailored support.

- **Cultural Competency Training** equips staff with the knowledge and tools needed to effectively engage with customers from diverse backgrounds.

- **Community Feedback Loops** allow for continuous collaboration with experts, ensuring service strategies remain responsive and relevant to the needs of diverse communities.

The impact of these celebrations on the office culture is profound. They have instilled a sense of pride and belonging among staff, who feel valued for their unique contributions and cultural identities. This pride extends to their interactions with customers, where they strive to create an environment of respect, dignity, and inclusivity. The celebrations have also enhanced teamwork, as staff members collaborate to make each event a success, learning from one another and building stronger relationships in the process.

Ultimately, the celebrations of diversity at the agency are not just about honoring different cultures, they are about embedding inclusive excellence into the very fabric of the organization. By continuously learning, adapting, and respecting the diverse needs of both staff and customers, the office exemplifies what it means to serve with integrity and compassion. This commitment to inclusive excellence ensures that every customer, regardless of their background, receives the highest standard of service, reflecting the true spirit of diversity and inclusion.

This highlights the connection between understanding colleagues' diversity and enhancing service to diverse customers, emphasizing how these celebrations foster a deeper appreciation and more effective service delivery.

A Rich Tapestry

Celebrating diversity involved recognizing and valuing the different perspectives and experiences that each customer brought. It was like imagining a tapestry woven from many different threads—each one unique in color or texture, contributing to the richness of the overall design. In customer service, this meant being open to different viewpoints and adapting approaches to meet diverse needs. By celebrating diversity, we not only enriched the customer experience but also built a more inclusive and supportive service environment.

Every human services agency I worked in provided opportunities to celebrate and honor the many diverse cultures, religions, and identities that made up our vibrant workplace and the communities we served. As I shared earlier, we took pride in recognizing days of significance such as Black History Month, Diwali, Pride Month, Indigenous Peoples Day, and various other important occasions throughout the year. These events weren't just moments of acknowledgment but were transformed into enriching experiences that brought our team closer together.

In all the human services organizations where I worked, I championed Diversity and Inclusion. I engaged with staff who identified with and celebrated different cultures, religions, or events, and encouraged them to take the lead in organizing those specific celebrations. For instance, during Pride Month, our 2SLGBTQIA+ colleagues led activities that highlighted their experiences and contributions, while during Diwali, staff who celebrated the Festival of Lights shared its significance and cultural richness with the team. A particularly beloved aspect of these celebrations was the sharing of food. Each event became a culinary journey, allowing us to taste and experience foods integral to different cultures—dishes many of us might never have had the opportunity to try otherwise.

Staff took immense pride in sharing their traditional foods, explaining the history and significance behind each dish. This not only enriched our palates but also deepened our appreciation for the diverse cultural tapestries that make up our team. Through these shared meals, we built connections and fostered a sense of unity, as we learned more about each other's backgrounds and the stories behind the flavors.

For bonuses go to ...

These regular celebrations, filled with the sounds, sights, and tastes of different cultures, foster a deeper understanding and respect for one another. They reinforce our commitment to inclusivity and create a supportive environment where everyone feels valued and recognized for who they are. By celebrating together, we not only enhance our workplace culture but also cultivate an atmosphere of appreciation and gratitude for the rich diversity that surrounds us.

The Power of Cultural Understanding

A traveler named Mrs. Patel (name changed), who had recently immigrated from India, came into the office seeking directions. She was headed to another city but had taken a wrong turn and found herself lost. With limited English and visible anxiety, Mrs. Patel seemed uncertain about what to do next. The receptionist, Nadia (name changed), who was familiar with Indian customs and culture, noticed her discomfort. Nadia greeted her with a respectful "Namaste" and a warm smile, which immediately put Mrs. Patel at ease. Nadia patiently gave directions, using simple language, visual aids, and a map to ensure clarity. By acknowledging Mrs. Patel's cultural background and adjusting her communication style, Nadia provided exceptional service. Mrs. Patel left the office feeling understood and respected.

Even though Mrs. Patel wasn't asking for a service directly offered by the organization, she was still treated as a customer—because anyone asking for help deserves support and compassion. The following day, on her way home, Mrs. Patel stopped by with her entire family, bringing a box of chocolates and a card which she left with the manager, to thank Nadia for the compassionate service she had received.

Celebrating This Success: As an organization, we celebrated Nadia's success in recognizing and respecting cultural differences by sharing her story in our internal newsletter. We also organized a cultural competency workshop where

Nadia shared her experience, helping to educate her colleagues on the importance of understanding and respecting the cultural backgrounds of our customers. This not only highlighted Nadia's exceptional service but also encouraged others to do the same.

Overcoming Language Barriers

A Spanish-speaking family arrived at the multicultural residential complex, clearly struggling with the English language. Having recently moved from Mexico, they needed help navigating the local system and finding family resources such as schools, doctors, and churches. Anna-Maria (name changed), a bilingual neighbor, overheard the conversation and voluntarily stepped in to assist. She greeted the family in Spanish, explained the process in their native language, and offered to guide them. She shared how, just a few years ago, she had been in the same situation, and a kind Spanish-speaking woman had helped her in a similar way. Wanting to repay the favor, Anna-Maria took extra time to ensure the family understood their options and the next steps they needed to take. She even connected them with a local community organization she was familiar with that offered additional support in Spanish. By breaking down language barriers and linking the family to vital resources, Anna-Maria not only provided exceptional service but also made the family feel welcome and valued in their new community. Neighbors are among the most important customers in our community.

Celebrating This Success: Anna-Maria became well known for referring people to this organization for assistance, and her effective handling of language barriers was celebrated by the agency she referred them to. They recognized her efforts by awarding her the "Diversity Champion of the Month" title. In response, the centralized program launched a new initiative to collect a list of all the languages spoken by its over 100 employees in many communities to better serve customers who did not speak English or French. During the award celebration, Anna-Maria's approach was highlighted, emphasizing the crucial role of communication in building trust and rapport with diverse customer groups.

Embracing Diversity in Gender Identity

A customer named Herbert (name change), who identifies as non-binary and uses they/them pronouns, visited the office to update their personal information in the system. The customer service representative, Jordan (name change), was aware of the importance of using correct pronouns and took the initiative to ask Herbert how they would like to be addressed. Jordan also ensured that the necessary changes were made in the system to reflect Herbert's gender identity accurately. By respecting Herbert's identity and making the process smooth and respectful, Jordan not only met but exceeded Herbert's expectations. This experience highlighted the significance of recognizing and embracing diversity in gender identity within customer service.

Celebrating This Success: Jordan's sensitivity and respect for gender identity are celebrated by creating a "Pride in Service" award, with Jordan being the first recipient. The organization also updates its training materials to include modules on gender identity and pronoun usage, ensuring all employees are equipped to provide inclusive service. Jordan's story is featured in a company-wide email, reminding everyone of the importance of recognizing and respecting each customer's identity, reinforcing our commitment to inclusivity.

Providing Emotional Comfort
Through Warmth and Patience

While the physical environment played a crucial role, the demeanor of the staff was equally important in creating a welcoming atmosphere. The office had trained all team members to greet each customer with warmth, patience, and understanding. This story followed Samantha (name changed), a front-line worker who exemplified this approach in her daily interactions.

One morning, an elderly customer named Desire Arnez (name changed) arrived at the office, visibly stressed and confused. She was struggling with the unemployment insurance application process after being recently laid off and felt overwhelmed by the paperwork. Samantha noticed her distress and immediately stepped out from behind the counter to greet Desire with a warm smile. She gently guided her to a comfortable seat and offered to help with the forms.

Samantha listened attentively as Desire explained her situation, offering reassurance and empathy. She took her time, connecting her with the online application and patiently walked her through each step of the process, making sure Desire understood and felt supported. Samantha's calm and kind demeanor helped alleviate Desire's anxiety, and by the end of the appointment, Desire felt more confident and less overwhelmed. She left the office with a sense of relief, knowing that she had been treated with love, respect and care.

Continuous Improvement and Staff Commitment

The commitment to creating a positive environment doesn't stop with the physical space and individual interactions. It's an ongoing effort that involves the entire team. The office regularly holds staff meetings to discuss ways to improve the customer experience. During these meetings, staff members share their observations and suggestions, ensuring that any potential barriers to comfort and accessibility are addressed promptly.

For instance, after noticing that some customers struggle with the length of time it takes to be served, the team decided to introduce a new queuing system that allows customers to check in via a kiosk and receive updates on their wait time. This change reduces anxiety and helps manage customer expectations, contributing to a more relaxed and comfortable atmosphere.

The story concludes with the impact these efforts have on the customers. Word spread throughout the community that this office is a place where people are not only served efficiently but are also treated with dignity and compassion. Customers feel comfortable coming to the office, knowing that their needs—both physical and emotional—will be met with care and respect.

A Commitment to Inclusion in the Educational System

As I observe the educational system today, I see the same patterns of exclusion I occasionally noticed in my childhood, children who self-isolate or are excluded by their peers. These moments resonate with me because I understand the long-term consequences of such isolation. Now, instead of just observing, I take action by offering a smile, kind words, or inviting these children to join activities. It's not only about kindness but also addressing exclusionary behavior directly, ensuring everyone understands that such actions are unacceptable. My goal is to foster an inclusive environment where every child feels valued and respected. These small acts of kindness and the willingness to call out inappropriate behavior are my way of planting seeds of inclusion, of letting these children know that they are seen, valued, and cared for. I want them to know that their presence matters, and that they don't have to navigate their school days feeling like they're on the outside looking in.

It's my hope that these gestures can help break the cycle of exclusion before it has a chance to take hold, offering these children a different path— one where they feel supported and encouraged to become the best versions of themselves. In doing so, I'm reminded of the power we each hold to make a difference in someone's life, simply by acknowledging their worth with a smile, a kind word, or by standing up against exclusionary behavior.

This emphasizes the importance of not only offering kindness but also actively addressing and calling out exclusionary behavior, reinforcing the commitment to creating an inclusive and supportive environment.

Top Three Takeaways

Every customer's voice matters. Wave your encouraging wand to turn their concerns into compliments, like the remarkably compassionate customer whisperer that you are.

Inclusive Excellence in Customer Service: Embrace diversity, inclusion, equity, and accessibility to create a welcoming environment. Acknowledging each customer's unique background fosters stronger relationships and positive interactions.

The Power of Positive Reinforcement: Use positive reinforcement, such as recognition and rewards, to enhance customer satisfaction and employee morale. This approach promotes service excellence and contributes to long-term organizational success.

Turning Challenges into Opportunities: By integrating empathy and personalized care, you can turn complaints into opportunities for growth. Addressing biases and promoting fairness helps build stronger customer relationships, advancing both personal and professional success.

Chapter 9
Building and Leading a
Customer-Centric Culture

"The secret of change is to focus all of your energy, not on fighting the old, but on building the new."
– Socrates, Greek Philosopher (479-399 BC)

9

The skills and talents of horse whisperers are often influences on the field of equine therapy. Equine therapy has been found highly beneficial for a wide range of therapeutic applications, from working with children with disabilities to helping heal teens with addictions and beyond.

Some horse whisperers claim that people have insights into their own behaviors and psyches when they work with horses in this kind of relationship. In many ways, what happens with the horse can trigger a connection to the person's behavior in life, allowing them to gain a deeper understanding of their reactions and decisions. The relationship someone in equine therapy has with their horse becomes a test relationship through which they can see their own behavior more closely, in order to effect change.

Extending the work of horse whisperers this way is how humans can benefit from equine therapy; it becomes a safe space where people can learn about how they judge themselves and others, what expectations they have of themselves and others, and what fears arise. There is no such thing as a bad horse, but there is such a thing as a fearful horse, and often the aggression and wildness a horse whisperer skillfully reigns, all comes down to taming that fear.

Leadership is at the core of success for a horse whisperer, and if they can be a trustworthy, resilient leader, they can then create a safe container for their horses. Horse whispering is more about understanding the horse than it is about riding it; similarly, customer whispering is about understanding the customer, not teaching them how to behave in a situation. When we are at our best, whether as leaders or horse whisperers, we can then influence the culture around us and elevate it to one of excellence.

Leading by Positive Example

Leadership is not just about giving orders, rather it is about setting the standard for others to follow. As a leader, your actions speak louder than words. When you demonstrate behaviors, traits, and attitudes that show competency and a commitment to exceptional customer service, your team is more likely to mirror that behavior. By showing respect, empathy, and dedication in your interactions, both with customers and with the team themselves, you inspire your team to do the same.

Both formal and informal leadership are essential to fostering a customer-centric culture. Formal leadership involves the official roles and responsibilities defined within the organizational structure, such as managers and supervisors. Informal leadership, on the other hand, arises when individuals influence others through their actions, attitudes, and behaviors, regardless of their official title. Both types of leadership are crucial in guiding staff and customers.

Furthermore, just as leaders guide their teams, customers look to front-line staff as leaders in their service experiences. Staff members are often seen as the decision-makers in their specific interactions, and their behavior can significantly influence customer satisfaction and trust. By modeling the organization's values and demonstrating a commitment to service excellence, staff can effectively lead customers through their service journey, ensuring positive and impactful interactions.

Leading by positive example also means holding yourself accountable. If your organization prioritizes customer satisfaction, you should be the first to address customer complaints promptly and thoroughly. Show your team how to turn complaints into opportunities for improvement and demonstrate the importance of following up to ensure issues are resolved to the customer's satisfaction.

Leading by positive example also means cultivating and subsequently demonstrating emotional intelligence. This involves recognizing and understanding your own emotions and those of others, using this awareness to guide your thinking and behavior, and adapting to different environments. Emotional intelligence fosters a positive work culture by promoting understanding, empathy, and effective communication. Additionally, building resilience through agile and nimble leadership is essential. This means demonstrating the ability to respond effectively and make challenging decisions when encountering volatile, changing, and uncertain organizational conditions. When employees understand the impact of their work on the customer experience, they are more likely to strive for excellence.

Over the course of my 50-year career in government and human services, with over 25 years in progressive leadership roles, my primary focus has always been on delivering exceptional customer service. While I have successfully led two major high-profile change projects—one that restructured a service delivery model to be more client-focused, involving the staffing of 350 employees and 22 managers across five offices, and another that streamlined operations and recovered significant funds from dormant cases—the initiative I am most proud of is a volunteer effort. This project clearly exemplifies the power of leading by positive example, which I'm excited to share with you.

As a dedicated volunteer with the JJ Murphy 4th Degree Knights of Columbus, I've had the unique opportunity to lead by example, not only through fundraising but by embodying the principles of *The Customer Whisperer: Turning Complaints into Compliments with the Wave of Your Wand*. The theme of building and leading a customer-centric culture resonates deeply with me. In this role, I've found that *the best way to find yourself is to lose yourself in the service of others*. Through my actions, I've fostered a culture of compassion, commitment, and service among the Knights, the Ladies, my family, Delta Bingo players, and everyone I influence.

As a dedicated volunteer with the "Ladies," I contribute to our fundraising efforts by fostering a customer-centric environment that transforms participation into a shared sense of purpose. The group has praised my involvement and recognized the positive impact of our collective work.

One of the most rewarding aspects of this work is seeing how our partnership with Delta Bingo & Gaming, which has raised over $500 million for local charities, directly impacts those in need. Our group, the JJ Murphy 4th Degree Knights of Columbus, supports approximately a dozen charities, including donating to various Catholic churches within our catchment area to contribute to their fundraising efforts. We also proudly support the Special Olympics, helping to enrich the lives of athletes with intellectual disabilities. By explaining how each game played at Delta Bingo supports these initiatives—whether it's contributing to local parishes, helping children's sports programs, or assisting Special Olympics—I've turned casual players into dedicated supporters, much like turning customer complaints into loyalty through care and connection.

Leading by example has meant more than just showing up for Delta Bingo events. It's about building relationships, sharing the impact of our work, and demonstrating the power of service. In line with the chapter on building and leading a customer-centric culture, I focus on empowering others to see how their involvement makes a difference. This approach is key to creating a positive environment where everyone—from my fellow Knights to the Delta Bingo players—feels valued and part of something bigger.

One of the most important organizations we support is the Saint Vincent de Paul Society, which, like the Knights, is dedicated to serving others with love, respect, justice, and joy. Our efforts help provide food vouchers to single adults, single parents, and families while also addressing other community concerns. By focusing on the needs of these vulnerable populations, I embody the customer-centric approach: understanding that each individual has unique challenges and that our role is to meet them with care, compassion, and solutions. It's about leading with empathy, much like I teach in my book—

meeting people where they are, acknowledging their needs, and finding ways to uplift them.

I've also seen how leading by example encourages the possibility of greater involvement in the future. While my efforts are dedicated to supporting the Knights in this particular charity, the Ladies actively engage in other charitable initiatives alongside them, working collaboratively to make a meaningful impact in the community. Each Knight contributes in a unique way, further advancing the organization's mission of service. Through our collective dedication, families and community members experience the fulfillment and sense of purpose that come from serving others. This commitment reflects the broader journey of fostering a customer-centric culture, where leadership rooted in integrity and compassion creates a ripple effect of positivity and service.

A memorable moment that encapsulates this was when a Delta Bingo player expressed doubt about how much her participation was helping. I took the time to explain how her involvement was supporting local women's shelters, food banks, and St. Vincent de Paul. By turning her doubt into understanding and pride, I transformed her experience—just as a leader in a customer-centric organization turns uncertainty into trust and commitment.

As I lead these efforts, I focus not only on raising funds but on building a culture of service within our group and the community. By consistently showing up, engaging with others, and leading with a positive attitude, I've fostered a team environment where everyone feels empowered to contribute. This aligns with the chapter's emphasis on *Leading by Example* and *Empowering Your Team*. Just as a customer-centric culture thrives on trust and empowerment, our fundraising efforts have grown stronger as more people recognize the value of their contributions.

Ultimately, leading by example has allowed me to live out the principle that *the best way to find yourself is to lose yourself in the service of others*. Whether we're raising funds for food vouchers, supporting women's shelters, contributing to the Special Olympics, or creating a positive environment for Delta Bingo players, every act of service builds a culture of care, compassion, and community. And just as in my book, where I teach how to turn complaints into compliments with the wave of a wand, here I wave my wand of leadership, transforming every effort into a celebration of service, gratitude, and lasting impact.

In the end, it's about more than just fundraising—it's about building a customer-centric culture within the Knights, the Ladies, and the community. By leading with compassion, inspiring others to serve, and always keeping the needs of those we help at the forefront, I've found not only myself but a deeper connection to those around me. And like the *Customer Whisperer*, I continue to wave my wand, turning every challenge into an opportunity and every interaction into a moment of shared purpose.

Over time in my career in human service, I progressively learned how to handle pressure and unexpected challenges with grace. It didn't happen overnight, and it certainly wasn't easy, but each experience brought me closer to mastering the art of staying calm in the face of adversity.

In my earlier years, I often felt overwhelmed by the fast pace of the work and the weight of responsibility. But as I gained more experience, I learned to pause before reacting. This became one of my most powerful tools. Initially, I didn't always have the luxury of stepping back, but over time, I realized that even a moment of pause can give you the clarity to make better decisions.

As I moved into leadership roles, I began to understand the importance of reframing challenges. Instead of seeing issues as problems to be fixed, I learned to view them as opportunities for growth. Whether it was resistance to a new staffing structure or labor relations tensions, each challenge became a chance to develop my skills and grow as a leader.

With time, I also learned to be kind to myself. In my early career, I was hard on myself when things didn't go as planned. But after facing many ups and downs, I came to understand that making mistakes is part of the learning process. I wasn't always calm, and I didn't always have the answers, but I learned to love and forgive myself, reflect on the situation, and use it as a steppingstone for future success.

Another lesson I gained progressively was the power of building relationships. Early on, I tried to handle everything on my own, but as I moved forward in my career, I recognized the value of leaning on others—whether it was my team, my peers, or external stakeholders. By fostering strong connections, I was able to tackle even the toughest situations with support.

Finally, patience became a key part of my approach. In the early stages of my career, I wanted immediate results, but over time, I learned that real change, whether in people or processes, takes time. When I faced resistance or setbacks, I trusted that with consistent effort, progress would follow.

Through this gradual development over my career, I came to understand that staying calm under pressure isn't something you're born with—it's something you learn, and I want readers to know that this kind of grace is within reach for them too. It's a journey of growth, patience, and learning to trust yourself in even the most unexpected situations.

For those of you who struggle with staying composed, here's what I've learned along the way:

- **Pause Before Reacting**: The space between a situation and your response is crucial. Taking a moment to pause allows you to respond with intention rather than impulse.

- **Reframe Challenges**: View obstacles as opportunities for growth. Shifting your mindset to ask, "What can this teach me?" can transform how you handle challenges.

- **Be Kind to Yourself**: Mistakes are inevitable. Learn to love and forgive yourself and move forward with wisdom, using each misstep as a learning opportunity.

- **Build Relationships**: Strong relationships with your team, peers, and partners can provide valuable support during tough times. Relying on others can make a big difference.

- **Patience is Key**: Real change takes time. Be patient and persistent, understanding that consistent effort leads to long-term success.

What I've learned over the years is that staying calm and composed is a skill you develop through experience. And if I can learn it, so can you. Be patient with yourself, give yourself the space to pause and reflect, and remember that grace comes with time and practice.

My ability to remain composed and solutions-focused in the face of adversity became a source of inspiration for my team. They saw that even in the most challenging times, excellence could still be achieved.

I led by example in every decision I made, demonstrating the values and standards I expected from others. My approach went beyond simply managing tasks. I nurtured a culture where team members felt valued and supported, by focusing on creating an environment where everyone felt heard, respected, and empowered. My understanding of team culture is rooted in the idea that it's not just about achieving goals but about how the team operates, communicates, and collaborates on a daily basis. A strong team culture is one where individuals feel a sense of belonging, where they trust each other, and where they know their contributions matter.

There were a couple of key things I did that proved to me that my team felt valued and supported:

- **Prioritizing Open Communication**: Through regular check-ins, one-on-one meetings, and team discussions, I ensured that everyone had a voice and felt their input was valued. This led to team members proactively offering innovative solutions without being prompted.

- **Empowering Ownership and Accountability**: By encouraging my team to take ownership of their work and trusting them to make decisions, I provided autonomy and resources that empowered them to lead confidently in their areas of expertise. This trust boosted their confidence and pride in their projects.

These actions showed me that when you invest in your team's well-being and development, they respond with dedication and a sense of ownership, which in turn strengthens the team culture.

This loving approach not only helped in keeping the project on track but also ensured that service to customers remained uninterrupted and of high quality.

I know that emotional intelligence has played a crucial role throughout my career, helping me navigate difficult situations with empathy, self-awareness, and calmness. I've learned to recognize my own emotions while also understanding and responding to the emotions of others. I'm aware of how my emotions impact those around me. This emotional intelligence has enabled me to build strong relationships, resolve conflicts, and lead with compassion, particularly in challenging environments.

I cultivated emotional intelligence over time by actively working on self-awareness and empathy. I had to learn to listen, not just to what people were saying, but to what they weren't saying—their body language, tone, and emotional cues. It was important to reflect on my reactions and ask myself why I felt a certain way in different situations. This self-reflection, combined with seeking feedback from others, helped me to grow.

If emotional intelligence is brand new to you, I'd say start by paying attention to your own emotions. When something happens that triggers a strong response, pause and ask yourself: "Why am I feeling this way?" From there, begin observing others—how do their emotions impact their behavior? Developing emotional intelligence isn't just about understanding others; it's about being in tune with yourself and using that insight to improve your interactions with others.

I definitely had some hiccups on my journey. Early on, I struggled with reacting too quickly to stressful situations. There were times when I would jump to conclusions or let frustration guide my responses. I had to learn how to pause before reacting and remind myself to step back, breathe, and assess the situation from a neutral standpoint. Another challenge was learning how to balance empathy with boundaries. I've always been someone who wants to help, but there were moments when I became too emotionally invested, which made it hard to stay objective. Over time, I learned how to be empathetic while still maintaining professional boundaries.

Cultivating emotional intelligence is an ongoing process, and the key is to be patient with yourself. It's a journey of growth, self-discovery, and learning how to better connect with others.

I was keenly aware of the emotional climate within the team and used this awareness to guide my interactions. When tensions rose, I was quick to address them, offering support and understanding. I adapted my communication style to meet the needs of different individuals, ensuring that everyone felt heard and respected. This approach fostered a sense of unity and purpose, helping the team stay focused on the goals of the project.

Thanks to our collective efforts, the project was successfully completed without disrupting customer services. The changes to the service delivery model and staffing structure were implemented smoothly, with the team emerging stronger and more cohesive than before. To mark this achievement, we organized a huge celebration on implementation day, bringing in executives to witness the success firsthand. This celebration was a moment of pride for everyone involved, as it not only recognized the hard work and dedication of the team but also solidified the positive relationships, we had built with labor representatives and community advocates.

My journey to becoming a leader was anything but smooth. It took me 10 years to move just one step up from an entry-level position, despite applying for countless jobs and going through interview after interview. Each time I faced rejection, it was a blow, but I didn't give up. I had a lot of lessons to learn along the way, and each setback was an opportunity for growth.

During those first 10 years, I realized that simply doing my job well wasn't enough. I needed to invest in myself if I wanted to move forward. So, I took courses, attended seminars, and engaged coaches who could help me develop the skills I needed. It wasn't easy balancing all of this with my day-to-day responsibilities, but I knew that persistence was key. Every course I took, every mentor I spoke with, helped me refine my approach and build the confidence I needed to take on new challenges.

When I finally made that first step up, I felt a sense of accomplishment, but the journey was far from over. It took another 10 years of continued learning, adapting, and growing before I moved into management. This phase of my career came with its own set of challenges. I had to learn how to lead by example, embrace change, and foster a culture where mistakes were seen as learning opportunities rather than failures.

One of the most important lessons I learned during this time was the value of visibility and agility. I made it a point to stay connected with my team, to be present and approachable, and to remain flexible in the face of change. But even more importantly, I learned that leadership isn't about having all the answers—it's about being open to learning and growing alongside your team.

For those who are new to customer service or leadership, I want you to know that it's okay to feel uncertain or even discouraged at times. My path wasn't perfect, and I made plenty of mistakes along the way. But each mistake taught me something valuable, and each rejection pushed me to try harder. The key is to keep going, to keep investing in yourself, and to trust that with time and effort, you'll get to where you want to be.

Looking back, it's clear that my journey was far from perfect. It was filled with setbacks, challenges, and a lot of self-discoveries. But what kept me moving forward was my commitment to learning, my persistence, and my willingness to embrace the lessons that each obstacle presented. For someone new to customer service or leadership, the road may seem long, but the growth that happens along the way is what shapes you into a strong, resilient leader.

The next generation of leaders learned from my example, understanding that true leadership is about more than managing tasks. It is about inspiring others to achieve their best while maintaining a focus on the needs of the customer.

Creating a Positive Environment

A positive work environment is the foundation of a customer-centric culture. Picture a garden where each plant is nurtured and cared for, leading to a vibrant and flourishing landscape. Similarly, a supportive and inclusive workplace encourages employees to thrive. Foster an atmosphere where feedback is constructive, teamwork is encouraged, and achievements are celebrated. This positive environment translates into better customer interactions and a more cohesive team.

In government services, we have a different take and context within which we serve our customers. So how might the positive work environment look in your small business, or in a large corporation?

Jeff Bezos is famous for leading his ten values with "customer obsession." As Amazon was growing, he and his team kept their eyes on that value and did everything they could to ensure the customer journey was positive and smooth from the moment they entered the website.

Websites are new environments, so creating a positive work environment even if your company is web-based can translate there, too. More and more we have teams spread out, working remotely, using apps like Zoom and Slack. Being creative and focusing on the values that matter, as well as cultivating a bit of that customer obsession-thinking that led Amazon to be among the top seven companies in the entire world, is a way of ensuring even your online business has the positive work environment that then ripples out to the customers through excellent service and support.

Vision, Mission, and Values

Building a culture in an organization is paramount to both the company's success and team loyalty, too. The foundation of a strong culture will always align with an organization's vision, mission and values. From there, behaving in ways that are consistent with these is crucial. If your organization's vision is to provide inclusive, innovative, responsive, and accountable service, your leadership should reflect these principles. If your company mission is to passionately deliver better services, boldly champion new ways of working, encourage new approaches to solving problems, and actively empower employees, then your leadership should also reflect these every day and in every interaction.

Some Customer-Centric Values

- **Integrity**: Acting with honesty and fairness in all dealings.

- **Respect:** Valuing diverse perspectives and treating everyone with dignity.

- **Excellence:** Striving for the highest standards in service and performance.

- **Accountability**: Being responsible for actions and outcomes and holding yourself and your team responsible for delivering on promises.

- **Innovation:** Encouraging creativity and new ideas for improving services, including encouraging your team to think outside the box.

- **Responsiveness:** Being attentive and adaptable to the needs of the community, promptly addressing customer complaints, and making necessary adjustments to prevent future issues.

- **Efficiency:** Maximizing resources to deliver the best possible service.

- **Trust:** Building confidence through transparency and reliability.

- **Collaboration:** Working together to achieve common goals.

- **Creativity:** Embracing new ideas to solve problems.

- **Fairness:** Ensuring equitable treatment for all.

- **Diversity:** Celebrating and valuing different perspectives and backgrounds.

- **Inclusion:** Engaging diverse employees to address their needs and advocate for inclusive policies by gathering feedback through forums and integrating it into service improvements.

These values play a significant role in building a world-class, modern workplace with dynamic leadership. They set the foundation for a positive and productive environment where employees feel valued and motivated to deliver their best work.

By aligning your behavior with the organization's vision, mission, and values, you create a cohesive and supportive work environment. Your team will see you as a reliable and trustworthy leader, and they will be more likely to emulate your commitment to excellence in their own roles.

Empowering Your Team

Empowering your team is key to leading and building a customer-centric culture. An empowered team is a team set up for excellence in customer service. After all, if your team supports customers, who supports your team? It is not unlike the oxygen-mask-scenario of self-care, wherein during any plane emergency the individual must put on their oxygen mask to help their neighbors. By leading in a way that empowers your team and establishing a culture to support this, you are ensuring everyone on the team has their oxygen mask on so they can give quality customer service. In short, empowering your team means giving them the tools, authority, and confidence to make decisions that enhance customer service. This involves several key strategies:

Foster a Culture of Leadership

A culture of leadership is one where everyone, regardless of their position, feels responsible for the customer experience. This culture is cultivated by recognizing and nurturing leadership qualities in all employees. Imagine a symphony orchestra where each musician contributes to the overall harmony. By encouraging leadership at every level, you create an environment where initiative and responsibility are valued, leading to a more dynamic and responsive service culture.

Creating a culture of leadership means instilling a sense of responsibility for the customer experience in every team member, regardless of their role. For example, imagine a customer service representative who notices a recurring issue with a particular product. Instead of just reporting it and moving on, they take the initiative to gather more information, suggest potential solutions, and collaborate with other departments to address the problem. This proactive approach is a direct result of a culture where leadership qualities are recognized and nurtured at all levels.

In a culture of leadership, every employee understands that their actions contribute to the overall customer experience. For instance, a warehouse worker who ensures that orders are packed accurately and shipped on time is as much a leader in their domain as a manager who oversees the process. By encouraging your team to step into leadership at every level, you create an environment that supports and celebrates taking initiative and responsibility.

When leadership qualities are fostered across the organization, it leads to a more dynamic and responsive service culture. Employees are more likely to go above and beyond for customers, finding innovative solutions to problems and continuously improving the service they provide. It's this collective commitment to leadership that strengthens the customer-centric culture you're striving to build, ultimately leading to greater customer satisfaction and long-term success.

Provide Comprehensive Training

Ensure your team is well-trained in all aspects of their roles. This includes not only the technical skills required but also training in soft skills such as communication, empathy, and conflict resolution. Regular training sessions and workshops help keep their skills sharp and relevant.

Encourage Open Communication

Foster an environment where team members feel comfortable sharing their ideas, concerns, and feedback. Regular team meetings, open-door policies, regular one-on-one conversations, and anonymous suggestion boxes can help create a culture of openness and trust. Keeping people informed about what we need to do to be successful and consistently delivering on organizational plans and priorities far beyond what is expected ensures that everyone is aligned and motivated.

Delegate Responsibility

Show trust in your team by delegating tasks and responsibilities. This not only helps distribute the workload but also empowers team members to take ownership of their work. Clearly define the scope of their authority and provide the necessary resources and support to carry out their duties effectively. Keeping people informed about what we need to do to be successful and consistently delivering on organizational plans and priorities far beyond what is expected ensures that everyone is aligned.

Involve the Team in Decision-Making

To foster a customer-centric culture, involving your team in the decision-making process whenever possible is quite crucial. This can be achieved through collaborative brainstorming sessions, forming committees focused on specific challenges, or creating task forces to address key customer service initiatives. For example, if your team is faced with the challenge of improving response times, gather them together to brainstorm solutions. By including diverse perspectives, you not only generate more creative ideas but also build a sense of ownership among your employees.

When employees feel that their voices are heard and their contributions matter, they become more invested in the outcomes. This sense of ownership leads to higher motivation and commitment to delivering exceptional customer service. Imagine a scenario where a task force is created to enhance the customer feedback loop. Employees who are part of this initiative will be more inclined to go the extra mile to ensure that the feedback gathered translates into actionable improvements.

By implementing these strategies, you create a team that is not only empowered but also motivated to excel. Empowered employees are more likely to take the initiative when faced with customer concerns, solve problems effectively, and contribute to a work environment that prioritizes customer satisfaction. For instance, a motivated employee might take it upon themselves to follow up with a customer after resolving an issue, ensuring the customer feels valued and their needs are fully met. This proactive approach strengthens the culture of excellence and customer focus that is essential to long-term success.

By implementing these strategies, you can create a team that is empowered, motivated, and capable of delivering exceptional customer service. Empowered employees are more likely to take initiative, solve problems effectively, and contribute to a positive and productive work environment.

Foster a Supportive Work Environment

The best way to grow a culture that is customer-centric is to always be supporting your front-line customer-facing staff. Part of this involves ensuring that you are creating a workplace culture in which your team members feel supported and respected. Address any issues of discrimination or harassment promptly and fairly. As much as you are able, try to promote work-life balance by being flexible with work schedules and offering resources for mental health and wellness. Provide the required employment accommodation to ensure that all employees can perform their best.

Recognition and acknowledgement of achievements, hard work, and even small daily successes goes a long way to maintaining a strong work culture that can support customers with excellence. Determine what your team responds to; some people love nothing more than being recognized publicly or accoladed with trophies and awards. But others prefer a private acknowledgement, or even just a simple thank you. Understanding your employees and how they respond to praise is another way of recognizing achievements appropriately while boosting morale, which then turns into motivation in the team. Celebrating achievements shows that you value their contributions and encourages them to continue striving for excellence.

Embodying Leadership Excellence

Excellence in leadership goes beyond simply managing tasks. It involves consistently demonstrating integrity and a genuine commitment to the organization's values. For example, if your organization prioritizes customer satisfaction, a leader who takes the time to personally address customer concerns, no matter how small, sets a powerful example for the team. This kind of leadership inspires trust and loyalty among employees because they see that their leader is not just talking about values but living them.

Imagine a scenario where there is a challenging situation, like a significant service disruption. As a leader, your team will have all eyes on you during your moment of response. We are always role models, and leaders especially. If you approach the situation calmly, take responsibility, and work collaboratively to resolve the issue, you are not just solving a problem, you are teaching your team how to act with integrity under pressure. As you lead with a focus on customer satisfaction, you are also leading by example in all aspects of your work.

Think of leadership excellence as being a beacon of light in a storm. Your team looks to you for guidance and reassurance during challenging times. By consistently demonstrating excellence, whether it's through ethical decision-making, clear communication, or a strong commitment to customer service, you set a benchmark for others to aspire to. This creates a ripple effect throughout the organization, where excellence becomes the standard, not the exception. It's this kind of leadership that not only drives a customer-centric culture but also fosters a strong, unified team dedicated to delivering the best possible service.

Inspiring Excellence in Service Delivery

Inspiring excellence in service delivery requires clear vision, motivation, and continuous improvement. Encourage your team to see every customer interaction as an opportunity to exceed expectations and provide them with the training and resources they need to excel. Recognize and reward exceptional service to reinforce the behaviors you want to see. Managing performance strategically involves giving constructive, compassionate feedback to individuals and groups.

When it comes to delivering feedback, ensure it is always done in a skillful way, considering how you might want to receive feedback yourself and with awareness of the vulnerability of the receiver. Giving feedback is an art that a strong leader will teach and role model, for example always padding any constructive criticism between two positive pieces of feedback.

When needed, engage your employees in improvement plans. Additionally, strive to build resilience through agile and nimble leadership. This means role modeling the ability to respond effectively and make challenging decisions when encountering volatile, changing, and uncertain organizational conditions. When employees understand the impact of their work on the customer experience, they are more likely to strive for excellence.

Top Three Takeaways

Lead with integrity and wave your wand to empower others and watch complaints melt into gratitude, like the inspiring, trusted, visionary customer whisperer that you are.

Lead by Example and Empower Your Team: Strong leadership and empowering your team to take responsibility for customer satisfaction are key to building a customer-centric culture. When leaders model the values they expect, they inspire outstanding service.

Foster a Positive Work Environment: Creating a positive work atmosphere and rewarding exceptional service boosts employee morale and leads to better customer outcomes, reinforcing a culture of excellence.

Implement a Systematic Approach to Cultural Change: A structured approach to embedding customer-centric practices ensures lasting success, benefiting both employees and customers and driving long-term success.

Chapter 10
Sustaining Excellence

"Without continual growth and progress, such words as improvement, achievement, and success Have no meaning."

— Benjamin Franklin

10

n a group home, nestled in a quiet neighborhood, the daily rhythm of care revolves around the residents with special needs, who call this place home. The staff here have long understood the profound impact of positive reinforcement on the residents' well-being and behavior. It's not just about meeting their basic needs, it's about creating an environment where they feel loved, valued, and understood.

The story begins with Emma (name changed), a gentle resident in her mid-thirties with a radiant smile that lights up the room. Emma loves routine and thrives on the little things that bring her joy, like the scent of fresh-baked cookies or the warmth of a soft blanket. The staff noticed early on that Emma responded exceptionally well to positive reinforcements, particularly when she was feeling anxious or overwhelmed.

When Emma completes a task, such as folding her clothes or helping to set the table for dinner, she is greeted with enthusiastic praise, a warm smile, and sometimes a small treat, like her favorite chocolate chip cookie. The positive reinforcement doesn't just end with a verbal acknowledgment; it's often accompanied by a gentle hug or cuddle, which Emma finds deeply comforting. Over time, this consistent and loving approach has transformed Emma's behavior, making her more engaged, confident, and willing to participate in daily activities.

This method of care, based on the principles of positivity and reinforcement, parallels the care we see in horse whisperers training frightened or wild horses, and what you are now learning to do as a customer whisperer. Just as the staff in the facility turned potentially challenging behaviors into positive outcomes by recognizing and rewarding good actions, you, as a customer whisperer, can transform complaints into compliments by acknowledging and addressing your customers' needs with empathy, understanding, and a proactive approach.

Positive Reinforcement Leads To Service Excellence

Imagine a customer expressing frustration over a service issue. By responding with compassion, addressing their concerns promptly, and perhaps even offering a small token of appreciation—a discount, a sincere thank you, or simply a warm smile—you can turn a negative experience into a positive one. This approach, much like the positive reinforcement used with Emma and the other residents, can significantly alter the outcome of the interaction. The customer, initially dissatisfied, feels valued and heard, which not only resolves their complaint but turns it into a moment of gratitude. In the same way that the home fosters a supportive environment through positive reinforcement, creating a culture of service excellence in your organization can have lasting benefits. By consistently delivering exceptional care and turning every potential complaint into a compliment, you build strong, positive relationships with your customers. This dedication to service excellence not only meets immediate needs but also creates long-term success through customer loyalty and glowing referrals. Similarly to how the residents thrived with positive reinforcement, your customers will respond positively when they feel appreciated and understood. This wave of your wand—your commitment to transforming complaints into compliments—becomes a powerful tool in creating memorable customer experiences and fostering a culture of excellence within your organization.

In the home, it was clear that the principles of positive reinforcement and service excellence aligned with a good customer service strategy. Keeping the focus on transforming challenges into opportunities for positive outcomes ultimately leads to greater satisfaction and success.

Positive reinforcement is a powerful tool in shaping behavior and fostering positive interactions. Acknowledging and rewarding positive customer interactions, such as saying "thank you," offering a small discount, giving a smile, or including a smiling emoji on a business card or email (if appropriate), can make customers feel valued and appreciated. Additionally, setting up a "kudos board" to publicly recognize excellent service can encourage positive behavior and foster a supportive work environment.

Service excellence benefits not only customers but also employees, leading to greater job satisfaction and fulfillment. Employees empowered to provide exceptional care experience increased morale and pride in their work, encouraging collaboration and reducing turnover. A positive work environment, where excellent service is valued and recognized, boosts morale and fosters a sense of pride in their work. This in turn encourages collaboration and teamwork, reducing turnover and enhancing overall organizational stability.

Throughout the book I have often mentioned the importance of creating memorable customer experiences, and it is true that doing this via delivering exceptional care can transform businesses. Picture a hotel that goes above and beyond to make guests feel welcome; the result is repeat business and glowing reviews. This dedication to customer satisfaction not only meets immediate needs but also creates long-term success through strong, positive relationships. The skills and positive attitudes developed through service excellence contribute to professional growth and career advancement, ultimately leading to a stronger brand and long-term success.

Learning from Feedback and Implementing Changes

Continuous improvement starts with learning from feedback. Customer feedback is invaluable, providing insights that help refine your service. Actively seeking and analyzing feedback ensures your service evolves to meet changing customer needs and expectations. Implementing changes based on this feedback demonstrates a commitment to improvement and responsiveness. This proactive approach builds trust and shows customers their opinions matter.

In 1995, I attended a self-improvement conference aimed at helping business owners refine their operations and customer service strategies. The conference room was filled with business managers and owners from various industries, all representing different regions and niches. The atmosphere was serious but collaborative, as everyone prepared to dive into the latest customer satisfaction surveys that had been gathered from across different locations.

The presenter stood at the front of the room, ready to lead the discussion. "Today, we're focusing on our customer satisfaction surveys across all regions," she began, gesturing to a large screen displaying a regional map with survey data. "Our goal is to detect any patterns and determine whether broader issues are affecting our service delivery."

As the data came into focus, it became clear that several regions were experiencing lower satisfaction scores, particularly in the area of service timeliness. "These trends suggest this might be a widespread issue, not just isolated to one or two locations," the presenter observed thoughtfully. "We need to take a deeper look to understand the root cause."

The team quickly began discussing possible reasons for the dip in satisfaction—staffing challenges, new processes that had been recently introduced, or even gaps in training. One of the coordinators suggested getting direct feedback from the staff at each location to better understand the obstacles they were facing and to gather more nuanced customer insights.

"We need to approach this systematically," the coordinator said. "Let's establish focus groups in each location to get input from our frontline teams. They can provide critical context to the customer feedback we're seeing in the surveys."

She continued, "Once we've gathered all the necessary information, we'll develop an action plan that not only addresses the immediate issues but ensures we maintain excellent service across all regions moving forward."

By the end of the meeting, the management team had set a clear timeline for gathering additional data and agreed to reconvene to finalize a comprehensive customer service action plan. I left that conference feeling inspired, knowing that by taking a step back to look at the bigger picture and addressing trends collaboratively, we could prevent minor issues from escalating and strengthen our commitment to delivering top-tier service. This experience reinforced my belief in proactive leadership and the importance of continuously improving how we serve our clients in my own business, Solutions Enterprises.

Implementing Changes and Continuous Review

After the initial conference, the team worked diligently over the following year to address the issues highlighted in the customer satisfaction surveys. Staffing levels were adjusted in areas where timeliness was a concern, filling vacancies to ensure smooth operations. Additional training was provided to equip all staff with the skills needed to handle updated processes. New customer service protocols were introduced, and frontline staff were encouraged to adopt a more proactive approach in their interactions with customers.

At the next year's conference, the presenter clicked through a series of slides displaying the latest data. "Initial reports show improvement," she announced. "Customer satisfaction scores have risen in most areas, particularly in the locations where we concentrated our efforts. However, continuous improvement requires more than just implementing changes—it's about ongoing review and adjustment."

The presenter paused to let the team absorb the data. "While overall progress is evident, some areas still need attention. For instance, although service timeliness has improved, we're seeing feedback that suggests some customers still feel they aren't fully heard or that their concerns aren't entirely understood."

She emphasized the importance of a continuous review process. "We must remain vigilant and responsive. Gathering feedback from both customers and staff regularly is critical. Our frontline staff can provide invaluable insights into what's working and where further improvement is needed."

To ensure continued success, the team agreed to establish a continuous review process. Regular feedback sessions would be held, where both customer and staff input would be closely analyzed. Adjustments would be made as necessary, with the understanding that the goal was not just to fix problems but to foster a culture of ongoing improvement.

As the presenter continued, she drew a parallel to the concept of a *Customer Whisperer*. "Like a skilled customer whisperer, we work behind the scenes, quietly waving our wand to turn complaints into compliments. While the public may not see the intricate efforts, we put into improving our service, the results are clear in the positive shifts in our customer satisfaction surveys."

"Continuous improvement is a journey, not a destination," the presenter reminded the group. "By staying adaptable and committed to learning from feedback, we ensure that our service evolves with the changing needs of our customers. This is how we sustain excellence—by turning feedback into action and transforming the customer experience, often without anyone noticing."

The meeting concluded with a renewed sense of commitment to not only implementing changes but also continually reviewing and refining them. The presenter recognized that by embracing this dynamic approach, they would continue to build trust with their customers, showing that their voices mattered. With a steady hand and an ongoing focus on improvement, they were confident that the quiet wave of their wand would lead to even more positive results in the future.

Employee Engagement Surveys

Many organizations, corporations, businesses, and various levels of government recognize that employee satisfaction is a key driver of overall success, which directly impacts customer satisfaction. To this end, they routinely measure employee satisfaction through surveys and other feedback mechanisms to identify areas of strength and opportunities for improvement. By understanding and addressing the needs and concerns of their employees, these organizations create a more motivated and engaged workforce, which in turn leads to better customer service and a more positive customer experience. This practice aligns with the principles we have articulated throughout the book, where fostering a satisfied and empowered employee base is essential for turning challenges into opportunities and achieving excellence in customer service. Through these efforts, organizations can ensure that they are not only meeting the needs of their internal workforce but also enhancing the satisfaction and loyalty of their external customers.

Surveys Sustain Excellence

Employee Experience Surveys are essential tools for measuring employee satisfaction, a critical factor that directly correlates with organizational success. When employees feel valued and supported, they are empowered to deliver exceptional service to external customers, who are often considered the organization's "first customers." Media reports and research from various sectors reinforce this idea, aligning with the core theme of *The Customer Whisperer: Turning Complaints into Compliments with the Wave of Your Wand* and the principles laid out in the chapter, "Sustaining Excellence."

The chapter emphasizes that *"Without continual growth and progress, such words as improvement, achievement, and success have no meaning."* This sentiment is reflected in how organizations continually work to foster employee satisfaction as a means to sustain excellence in service. Recent media shows that organizations that prioritize employee recognition, support, and well-being see measurable improvements in customer service outcomes. A positive workplace environment, strong leadership, and work-life balance are key contributors to higher employee satisfaction, which in turn leads to faster response times, better customer interactions, and more positive feedback—elements that align perfectly with the book's sub-sections, "Positive Reinforcement Leads to Service Excellence" and "Learning from Feedback and Implementing Changes."

For instance, Gallup research demonstrates that organizations with high employee engagement report 21% higher profitability and 17% better productivity. In addition, businesses that experienced a 10% increase in employee engagement often saw a 5-8% improvement in customer satisfaction. This trend is seen not only in the private sector but also in the public sector, where companies such as a global retail chain with high employee engagement levels reported faster response times and a 15% boost in customer satisfaction. Similarly, in the healthcare sector, an 8% rise in patient satisfaction was linked to a 12% increase in employee engagement, illustrating how positive reinforcement directly contributes to service excellence.

Public sector data from multiple government organizations align with these findings and the sub-section "Implementing Changes and Continuous Review." The 2022 Employee Experience Surveys conducted by various governments revealed valuable insights into employee engagement, satisfaction, and workplace culture. Though some organizations saw a slight dip in engagement compared to 2021, many reported higher engagement levels than in 2019, with nearly half of employees reporting high satisfaction. These surveys underscored the importance of motivation, job satisfaction, and leadership—all of which are critical for delivering high-quality service to external customers. This is a clear reflection of the book's focus on "Learning from Feedback and Implementing Changes" as a key to sustaining excellence.

In both public and private sectors, fostering inclusivity, fairness, and diverse opinion expression contributes to a positive work environment. Leadership, while generally effective, showed areas for improvement, such as aligning words with actions. Surveys also revealed the need to address workload, work-life balance, and stress management, all of which are essential for maintaining employee motivation and ensuring ongoing excellence in customer service. These findings emphasize the importance of continuously reviewing employee engagement to identify areas for growth, a direct parallel to the book's focus on "Implementing Changes and Continuous Review."

Overall, these insights highlight that, as outlined in *The Customer Whisperer*, employee engagement is not a one-time effort but a continual process. By gathering feedback, implementing changes, and fostering a positive work environment, organizations can create a cycle of improvement that sustains both employee and customer satisfaction. Whether in the private sector, healthcare, or government, a satisfied and motivated workforce is the key to delivering exceptional service and turning challenges into opportunities—ensuring that improvement, achievement, and success are continually realized.

Through this continuous growth, organizations can truly embody the philosophy of *The Customer Whisperer* by transforming customer interactions from complaints into compliments, all while maintaining and sustaining excellence in service delivery.

Celebrating Successes and Maintaining High Standards

Acknowledging and celebrating successes is crucial for maintaining motivation and morale. Celebrating both small and large achievements fosters a culture of appreciation and continuous improvement. Consistent service quality involves practical steps like establishing clear standards, providing ongoing training, and regularly reviewing performance. Sustaining high standards requires continuous effort, regular evaluations, and adapting to new challenges, ensuring your service remains top-notch over time.

Recognizing and celebrating achievements are key practices within organizations of all sizes. These traditions not only boost morale but also reinforce the values and goals that drive excellence within a workplace. Whether it's a simple "Employee of the Month" award or a more elaborate recognition program, such practices are essential in nurturing talent and motivating employees to continue performing at their best.

Prominent organizations like Starbucks and McDonald's use "Employee of the Month" programs to acknowledge and reward individual contributions, ensuring that exceptional efforts are celebrated. Similarly, Google has cultivated a culture where employees can give peer-to-peer bonuses, fostering an environment of appreciation and teamwork. At Disney, the prestigious "Disney Legacy Award" honors cast members who embody the company's values, highlighting their contributions to creating magical experiences.

Even smaller organizations recognize the importance of acknowledging excellence, whether through thank-you notes, annual ceremonies, or other forms of recognition. These efforts, no matter the scale, are crucial in maintaining high standards and encouraging continuous excellence.

The Ontario government is committed to recognizing excellence both within and outside its organization. Through a variety of awards, the government celebrates the contributions of individuals, groups, and external partners who go above and beyond to improve lives and strengthen communities across the province. From internal recognitions like the Amethyst Award to external honors such as the Ontario Volunteer Service Award, these initiatives reflect the government's dedication to fostering a culture of excellence, inclusivity, and service.

Other levels of government follow a similar approach, with federal, provincial, and municipal bodies across Canada recognizing both internal employees and external stakeholders for their contributions. Awards like the Ontario Medal for Good Citizenship and the Premier's Awards for Excellence in the Arts further demonstrate the emphasis on collaboration and partnership in enhancing public service and community development.

Recognition plays a crucial role in fostering a culture of excellence, as highlighted in *The Customer Whisperer: Turning Complaints into Compliments with the Wave of Your Wand*. In alignment with the book's theme of *sustaining excellence* and *celebrating successes*, the Ontario government exemplifies this through its Annual Employee Recognition Award ceremonies, held across various ministries. These events are more than just formal gatherings; they represent the ministry's commitment to maintaining high standards and recognizing the dedication, leadership, and innovation of its employees.

Hosted by senior leaders such as the Deputy Minister or Assistant Deputy Minister, the ceremony celebrates achievements in categories such as Customer Service Excellence, Teamwork, Innovation, Leadership, Diversity & Inclusion, and Sustainability Initiatives. Special recognition is given to long-term service, with employees who have dedicated 20, 25, 30 years, or more being honored for their enduring commitment. This formal recognition reinforces the ministry's dedication to continuous improvement and high performance.

Beyond these annual ceremonies, recognition is woven into the daily operations of the ministry. Managers regularly acknowledge their team members with praise, kudos emails, and informal gestures of appreciation. Smaller, unit-level events further ensure that employee motivation is kept fresh, emphasizing the importance of consistently maintaining high standards. By celebrating achievements and rewarding dedication, the ministry ensures that success is not just a one-time event but an ongoing process. This aligns with the book's focus on *sustaining excellence*, turning challenges into opportunities for growth and fostering a culture that continuously strives for improvement. Recognizing success is key to maintaining momentum and driving organizational success, ensuring that employees feel valued and motivated to continue delivering their best.

Leveraging Technology

Leveraging technology for better service delivery has become a cornerstone of modern customer service across various levels of government and organizations. As John Lasseter once said, *"The art challenges the technology, and the technology inspires the art."* Technology enhances service by streamlining operations, improving response times, and providing valuable insights that help organizations tailor their services to the evolving needs of customers.

Governments at all levels—federal, provincial, and municipal—along with private organizations, are increasingly using technology to offer more efficient and accessible services. For instance, Ontario's Ministry of Transportation (MTO) has adopted digital services to simplify tasks like renewing driver's licenses, paying for road tolls, and updating vehicle registrations online, saving customers time and reducing service bottlenecks. Similarly, the Federal Government's platforms, such as those for Old Age Security (OAS), the Canada Pension Plan (CPP), and Employment Insurance (EI), leverage technology to offer Canadians 24/7 access to essential services. Ontario's social services' MyBenefits app has transformed how residents interact with caseworkers and manage their benefits. This app allows users to submit documents, track payments, and manage appointments—all from their smartphones—significantly improving efficiency and reducing frustration.

This type of innovation is also seen in private sectors like insurance, where companies such as SunLife and Canada Life offer apps that enable customers to manage claims, view benefits, and access support services seamlessly. Other sectors, like healthcare and financial services, are also leveraging technology.

Telemedicine platforms now allow patients to consult with healthcare providers remotely, enhancing access to care, particularly in underserved regions. Similarly, financial institutions have integrated AI-powered chatbots into their service models, providing instant support for transactions and resolving customer issues in real-time. Retail companies have been using data analytics for years to personalize customer experiences, offering tailored recommendations based on shopping history, which enhances customer satisfaction and loyalty. While digital tools enhance convenience and accessibility, they do not replace the importance of human connection, empathy, and personalized service. Technology provides tools that help organizations serve customers better, but human interactions remain crucial for delivering exceptional service, especially when addressing complex or sensitive issues. No AI or app can replicate the compassion and nuanced understanding that come from direct human-to-human engagement.

The use of technology also aligns with the core principles of *The Customer Whisperer: Turning Complaints into Compliments with the Wave of Your Wand*, particularly in the chapter on sustaining excellence and celebrating successes. By staying ahead of technological trends, governments and organizations build trust and demonstrate their commitment to continuous improvement. For example, apps like MyBenefits and the CPP/OAS platforms reflect a commitment to evolving with customer needs and turning potential frustrations into positive experiences, much like the customer whisperer approach transforms complaints into compliments. Incorporating these innovations ensures that services remain relevant, adaptive, and efficient, creating a personalized experience for customers. This helps organizations build long-term trust, as customers know they are not only getting immediate solutions but also benefiting from a team committed to excellence and sustained service quality.

By leveraging technology, whether through government programs or private sector innovations, we embrace the spirit of continuous improvement and service excellence. As we observe best practices across various sectors, from healthcare to finance, we reaffirm our dedication to adopting cutting-edge technologies that further enhance our ability to provide top-tier service while maintaining the irreplaceable value of human connection. This blend of technology and personalized service enables organizations to fulfill the promise of *The Customer Whisperer* by turning challenges into opportunities and delivering lasting customer satisfaction.

Building a Legacy of Customer Satisfaction

The vision of building a legacy of customer satisfaction must become central to any customer-facing business, government service or organization. To become the most trusted and customer-centric company in your industry, you must provide your team with a powerful direction and invite them into that shared goal. For example, aiming for a 95% customer satisfaction rate within a two-year period not only aligns with this vision but also sets a measurable target for excellence. Staying ahead of trends by incorporating the latest customer service technologies, like AI-driven chatbots, ensures you consistently meet and exceed customer expectations.

Preparing your team for challenges, such as training them to handle high-stress situations during peak seasons, maintains the high standards necessary for this legacy. By focusing on these elements, you don't just maintain excellence, you build a lasting reputation that defines your legacy of customer satisfaction that endures beyond individual transactions. By consistently delivering outstanding service, you build a reputation for excellence that attracts and retains customers.

Kindness Matters

For centuries, horse whispering techniques were used by Indigenous populations. These people understood and respected the fact that they were in a relationship with these remarkable beasts. Horse whispering in many ways evolved out of a natural horsemanship approach that sought to keep the relationship as the focal point, allowing horse and human to develop a bond. The best, and most long-lasting way, to develop that bond – a bond based on mutual love, respect, trust and safety—remains horse whispering, to this day.

In the business and government services world, customer whisperers act like horse whisperers in every interaction. It is the focus on the relationship that matters most, and as the world continues evolving, the need for this focus to return in a prominent way could not be clearer. While technology is certainly helping us, it is also dividing us. For every company opting to use chatbots and community forums instead of keeping humans on the phone for customer service, there is now increasingly a company doing the opposite, remembering that human-to-human contact is still how relationships are built, and relationships are at the heart of what we do.

As you journey deeper into the heart of customer whispering, carry with you the essence of the principles I've shared in this book. Remember that the best customer service happens when you are fully present listening with empathy, acting with kindness, and genuinely committed to meeting each customer's needs. It's not about perfection but about the human touch you bring to every interaction. When you serve from a place of compassion and care, you not only elevate the customer experience, but you inspire those around you to do the same.

You already have everything you need to be an excellent customer whisperer. Trust in your ability to make a meaningful difference in the lives of others, one interaction at a time. With every challenge you transform into an opportunity, you're creating ripples of positivity that extend far beyond the moment. Your dedication, your heart, and your commitment to service excellence will set you apart and leave a lasting impact.

So go forward with confidence, knowing that you have the power to turn complaints into compliments, to turn moments of frustration into moments of connection, and to inspire others through your actions. You can do this, and the world is waiting for the unique magic you bring to customer service."

Top Three Takeaways

Continuous Improvement and Learning: Regularly assess and improve customer service practices by learning from feedback, implementing changes, and celebrating successes to maintain excellence.

Leveraging Technology for Enhanced Service: Embrace technology to increase service efficiency and personalization, providing better customer experiences that meet evolving needs.

Building a Supportive Environment for Long-Term Success: Foster a supportive work environment to sustain momentum, prevent burnout, and maintain high standards for lasting customer satisfaction and positive experiences.